Living Black

Living Black

Social Life
in an African American Neighborhood

Mark S. Fleisher

The University of Wisconsin Press

The University of Wisconsin Press
1930 Monroe Street, 3rd Floor
Madison, Wisconsin 53711-2059
uwpress.wisc.edu

3 Henrietta Street, Covent Garden
London WC2E 8LU, United Kingdom
eurospanbookstore.com

Printed in the United States of America

Library of Congress Cataloging-in-Publication Data

Fleisher, Mark S., author.
Living black: social life in an African American neighborhood / Mark S. Fleisher.
pages   cm
Includes bibliographical references.
ISBN 978-0-299-30534-5 (pbk.: alk. paper)
ISBN 978-0-299-30533-8 (e-book)
1. African Americans—Illinois—Champaign—Social conditions.
2. Ex-convicts—Illinois—Champaign—Social conditions.
3. Gang members—Illinois—Champaign—Social conditions.
4. Ex-gang members—Illinois—Champaign—Social conditions.
I. Title.
E185.86.F56   2015
305.896'073077366—dc23
2015008381

To the memory of
Professor Irving Spergel.

Irv's kindness, patience, and thoughtfulness
enriched the years we worked together.
I miss his laughter and smile.

Contents

Acknowledgments
ix

Prologue
3

1. The Ethnographer and the Ex-Convict
7

2. Culture and Social Life
22

3. Lively Streets
33

4. Everyday Life
51

5. New Neighbors
67

6. Dreams and Realities
85

7. Rebirth Days
104

8. They Don't Need a Savior
124

Epilogue
129

Notes
135
References
155

Acknowledgments

Living Black expresses the cultural vibrancy and resilience of a black community known as the north end among folks in Champaign, Illinois. Personal lives and challenges faced by north end residents are represented and expressed through the lives of the Washington family and a man who calls himself Burpee. In opening up their homes and permitting me to sit in their living rooms and share their meals, they and many of my other north end friends allowed me to witness the struggles, rewards, and joys of their lives. Their generosity over many years has made possible this ethnographic depiction of the north end that counters racial stereotypes of life in a poor black community and documents the enduring symbiotic relationship between the residents of the north end and the largely white community and local police departments.

This book relies upon ethnographic data gathered in good faith, with the consent of the individuals under observation, and with as much accuracy as possible. Some personal details, place names, and distinctive details of events in this book's text were altered for the protection and preservation of the rights of the individuals. In no case did I intentionally slander or in any way injure the repute of individuals, private entities, or government agencies. I presented my own observations and my own analysis. Opinions expressed in this book do not represent the official position or policies of the U.S. Department of Justice and its Office of Juvenile Justice and Delinquency Prevention, the U.S. Census Bureau, Illinois State University, or Case Western Reserve University or its trustees.

Living Black

Prologue

Living Black chronicles the personal lives of real people who reside on the north end, a small black community established in Champaign, Illinois, in the early years of the twentieth century.[1] The historical significance of the north end was its location, straddling the intersection of north-south and east-west branches of two railroads, which carried descendants of slaves to northern urban centers like Detroit and Chicago and to smaller communities in Ohio, such as Cleveland and Youngstown. Chicago's proximity to Champaign has meant that gangs and violence are prevalent in the north end, a record of which can be found in the folkloric accounts of their history that north end people give.

When I arrived on the north end in the mid-1990s and began my work as a local evaluator on a national youth gang suppression, intervention, and prevention initiative, folks referred to the north end as Little Chicago, an indicator of the continuous migration between Chicago's south side and rural Champaign. I spent six years doing research on the north end as part of three federally funded research projects.[2] Over those years, my field research guide was a middle-aged career criminal and recidivist who called himself Burpee. In the early weeks of research, he escorted me to the Pines, a public housing project on the north end, where he introduced me to the Washington family, a gregarious family he thought would be a good starting point for my research, knowing that several family members were or had been members of the Vice Lords street gang.

Burpee introduced me to the lady of the house, Maureen "Mo" Washington, and her husband, James "Memphis" Washington, as well as their teenage sons, Calvin, Bennie, and Willie, and their teenage daughters, LaWanda and Iresha. Jason, their eldest son, was in prison. I met him years later. A heated argument over a $15 gambling debt resulted in the death of the family's second eldest son, Big C. Neighbors described the scene: "Mo found 'im dead, oozing blood. No one nearby in the housing project said they heard the nine-millimeter handgun blast a hole in Big C's chest. Stunned, his two young brothers and sisters saw mom kneeling over his shattered body. Neighbors in the Pines huddled near Mo, heads shaking, mouths mumbling in disbelief. There he was, Big C, a well-liked teenager murdered in daylight on the common area between rows of apartments."

Living Black narrates, in their own words, the story of the Washington family's struggle with personal loss, Big C's murder, and Mo and Memphis's dream of the day when their children would escape the cultural boundaries of the north end. Iresha dreamed that she'd play basketball for the women Wolverines of the University of Michigan. Bennie and Willie anticipated that one day they'd be freshman strolling on a glorious university campus, like the one nearby. LaWanda dreamed that her son would have a stable family life. Their pleasant dreams were confronted by the reality that their bigoted brother Jason was soon to be paroled after his second term in prison and would return home, only to disrupt family life and bring trouble to their door again.

Living Black documents the intimate lives of Burpee and Big C's family and describes Burpee's role as a legitimate—a well-respected and accepted—member of the north end community, after his lifelong struggle with crime and addiction and six terms in prison. The story describes the adventure that comes along with walking into a poor black community, meeting people who agree to help a stranger—a university professor, a white man—complete a research assignment, and the blossoming of my relationship with Burpee and the Washington family.

Things I saw, people I met, things I did, and things I have learned are not told here like they might be in a magazine story that wearily depicts a downtrodden, crime- and drug-ridden, impoverished black slum battling discrimination and racism. This story of Champaign's north end community chronicles the symbiotic relationship between north end citizens, the local police departments, and the predominantly white citizenry of Champaign-Urbana, describes the ways north end people squeezed the best of life out of modest surroundings and enriched their lives with social ties to family and friends, and illustrates that, in spite of economic scarcity over the past century, north end residents created and sustained a spirited community.

On the north end, privation didn't overshadow the good things of life. There were an abundance of children who were celebrated with birthday parties, cake and candles and gifts, and always plenty of laughter. National holidays elevated folks' spirits. Early on Thanksgiving morning one year, my son and I visited Dorothia, the Washingtons' neighbor at the Pines, who stood at her sink, smiling and giggling and chatting, while she cleaned a mound of chitterlings in anticipation of the arrival of her Chicago family to her home for a family dinner. Behind her, taped on the refrigerator door, was a picture of her husband posing in the visiting room of a federal prison; every day, she said, he is one day closer to coming home.

North end families overcame personal tragedies like the murder of a son and coped with absentee landlords, inadequate housing, deficient medical care, and limited transportation to employment sites, problems commonly encountered by whites, blacks, and Hispanics in poor communities across the country. Old houses, weed-ridden lawns, streets cluttered by soda cans and cigarette butts gave a look of poverty to the north end, yet it wasn't a dangerous and socially unhealthy community plagued by chronic violence and life-threatening disease like communities I had studied outside the United States. I've done cross-cultural research in truly deplorable places, where infant mortality rates were sky-high, where there were no health care facilities or clinics were so distant that folks who needed care were unable to reach them, where potable water was only occasionally accessible, and where insufficient nutritious food contributed to childhood malnutrition and disease. The north end had a far superior quality of life than those desolate places.

Living Black documents north end poverty in its material form and describes how folks use social networks to manage privation. I am not an expert on cultural and structural conditions of poverty in American

African American communities. I have no scholarly voice in legislative debates on social policies that affect the poor. I have no academic standing in the policy arena. I have not published books on the social policy mechanics of fixing poverty. My professional role in the public debate on poverty has been limited to the observations and firsthand descriptions of real-life conditions poor people encounter and how they adapt to those conditions.

The takeaway of *Living Black* is that people like Burpee and the Washingtons and their north end neighbors earn incomes, start families, develop friendships, and manage their households abiding by their culture's vision of normal lives, that the quality of life on the north end depends more on rich social interactions and support networks than on income, that outsiders like you can learn to look past your culture-bound worldview—your judgment of the way other folks like those on the north end live their lives—that north end folks are quite able to resolve their own dilemmas without outside intervention, and most importantly, that you can learn to respect cultural differences.

1

The Ethnographer
and the Ex-Convict

I am a cultural anthropologist, an ethnographer.[1] I study human behavior in cultural contexts and describe the way people live day to day by getting knee-deep in their communities over long periods. To account for their behavior, I reveal unwritten cultural rules that mold people's thoughts and influence their interpretation of the world around them. I've applied the research methods of a cultural anthropologist to communities both outside and inside the United States. In Mexico I lived among Otomi peasants, in the Netherlands I walked among Moroccan street gangs, and in the Guatemalan highlands I collaborated with linguists and anthropologists on a linguistic education project among Mayans. I have done participant observation on community life in Istanbul, Turkey. I have spent years among native people in British Columbia and American Indians on the northwest coast of the United States. I have done ethnographic research among youth gang members on the streets in Seattle, Washington, Kansas City, Missouri, and East Cleveland, Ohio. I have been an observing participant in cellblocks of a federal penitentiary as a correctional worker.

When Burpee, an ex-convict I met in the north end of Champaign, Illinois, asked me what an anthropologist does, I told him about those forty years of field research studies.[2] Those research experiences mattered little to Burpee. To him, I was a stranger, a white man. Burpee classified strangers first by color, then by their experience with crime and prison. The kind of people he had known were on Chicago's streets and in Illinois's prison cellblocks. The people who meant most to him were black gang members who had extensive criminal and prison histories. They were the people he most respected. They were his primary reference group, the people he had an intuitive understanding of, people whose dilemma as ex-cons he could easily grasp.

Burpee and I met on a panel discussion about youth gangs televised on the public television station at the University of Illinois at Urbana-Champaign. I was introduced as an expert on gangs. That introduction infuriated him because I was racially and radically different from his primary reference group. I am not black. I have never been a gang member. I have never been a prison inmate. I was as strange a stranger as he'd ever met. In his way of thinking, I had not earned the privilege of talking with authority about gangs. Real gangsters, Burpee said, paid their dues by perpetrating street crime and violence and by doing jail and prison time. Burpee had scars to prove his firsthand acquaintance with violent street life. A white man, a college professor, had no right to talk about men like him. My role on the television gang panel was tantamount to a slap in the face, an insult to men who earned the right to tell viewers about gangs, the Real Gangsters.

Burpee might have looked past my criminal inexperience if I had not been a white man. Race mattered at that moment on the television panel. He grew up on Chicago's south side in the 1950s and 1960s when blacks were vilified, rejected, spurned. His distrust, dislike, and enmity toward white men fifty years later wasn't rational, although his feelings seemed reasonable given his socialization into a world dominated by white citizens who hated blacks.[3]

Despite how he felt at the time we met, I needed his help. We struck up a business relationship that lasted six years. I was the first white man he had known who asked him for something other than cocaine or street insurance to protect themselves from predators like him. Over time, his view of me shifted. I went from being a white man whose very presence insulted him to a guy willing to let him teach me about street life. My skin color became less important to him as time passed. The day he referred to me as "the White Man," I knew our relationship was amicable, for the moment.[4] Only near the end of our relationship, six years later, when my white skin faded out of his view, did he call me Mark. Otherwise, he called me "Joe," a moniker he used for all white men.

We worked together on each of my research studies on the north end. Months passed, we got to know each better. I confused him. "Why would a white man, a college professor, want to hang out in the 'hood interviewing young gangsters?" he wondered. My time, he thought, would be better spent talking to real gang members, gangsters like him. The north end had dozens of adult gangsters allegedly retired from their gangster ways with long criminal histories and decades of time inside prison. Burpee called them "old gangsters in retirement." Even in retirement, he said, old gangsters like to stay on their hustle a bit longer. The longer I hung around, the more I learned how easily retired gangsters slip back into illegal ventures, albeit safer ones, like managing transportation conduits for the distribution of illegal drugs across the northern central states. The story of the north end, Burpee, and the Washington family began with a phone call in 1995.

The Call

"Hello?"

"Is this Professor Fleisher?"

"Yes."

It was Professor Irving Spergel at the School of Social Service Administration at the University of Chicago.[5] He said he needed a local evaluator in Bloomington, Illinois. We discussed details of a local evaluator's responsibilities, and I agreed to join the project. Bloomington was one of five target cities across America, chosen through a competition, where a youth gang suppression, intervention, and prevention demonstration project sponsored by the U.S. Justice Department's Office of Juvenile Justice and Delinquency Prevention was to be implemented.[6] Target sites were matched to comparison sites, like a statistical eHarmony community matchup. Bloomington was a match with Champaign with respect to numerous demographic variables.

Target sites like Bloomington were deluged with social services for adolescent gang members and their families, in the hope that they'd stop running the streets, finish school, get a job, settle down, and stop doing the things that got them arrested. Part of my job at the target site was interviewing adolescent gang members chosen by Bloomington's local agencies.

Champaign is located in the cornfields of central Illinois about 55 miles southeast of Bloomington, 90 miles southeast of Peoria, 120 miles southwest of Chicago, and 160 miles northeast of East St. Louis. My responsibilities in Champaign included conducting interviews with adolescent gang members whose demographic, social, and criminal histories matched those of adolescents in Bloomington. I had to select these adolescent gang members myself and had no idea where to find them and did not know anyone who could introduce them to me.

The Locale

I saw Champaign for the first time in 1993. The town seemed oddly out of place, though, like magic seeds had been dropped from the sky into the center of an agricultural field that sprouted a town and a university. Over several years in the mid-1990s I had become familiar with Champaign when I drove my son to his gymnastics practice facility, which was located on the northern edge of the business area and the southern edge of a poor neighborhood. That neighborhood didn't have the look of a tough place. Later I learned it was the north end. When my research ended and I drove out of Champaign in 2002, the campus had new libraries, laboratory buildings, and dorms, and the town had new shopping centers, restaurants, motels, movie theaters, and bars and more bars that had sprouted quicker than crabgrass on a spring lawn.

Towns like Champaign harbor well-educated people under the camouflage of commerce. Green Street traverses campus east to west and is lined by bars, fast-food joints, ice cream dispensaries, ethnic food shops and restaurants, and a cigar shop with glass cases that display fine cigars and pipes and tobacco products. The cigar shop was one of my favorite hangouts; I would enjoy a cigar and listen to locals talk about goings-on around town. An $8 cigar tendered by a retired physicist or poet laureate or by the pipe-repair fellow, a forty-something, long-time resident with a master's degree in literature from the university down the street, bought a ticket to a gossip forum. Smokers wandered in, lit up, and stayed a while, talking nonstop about sports, politics, local news, and things about the town that bothered them. No one talked about gangs. Neither did parents at my son's gym, locals at coffee shops, or guys drinking draft beers at pubs.

Until Spergel called me, I had no reason to think about gangs in Champaign and Urbana. I saw no evidence of youth gangs on or near the north end. The idea of drive-by shootings, brawls in the park, and illegal drug sales simply didn't comport with the ambience of that rural college town.

Fear and Trepidation

Spergel's project staff at the University of Chicago helped Bloomington personnel set up the project there. There were no project personnel to help me set up gang member interviews in Champaign. I was the setup man. Setting up a grant-funded project requires collaboration with community officials, police departments, and local neighborhoods. Field research requires working the streets and dealing with local folks.

I had an obligation to interview no fewer than one hundred gang members a year and to reinterview the same gang members over the next two to three years. I had to be sure the police knew I wasn't a drug dealer or drug customer or street hustler. When I agreed to work on the project, I had no idea where to find the police stations. I had no personal or professional history with local police chiefs. I didn't know where to find gang members. Two first steps were in order. Find the police. Find the gangs.

A street researcher can rush into town and somehow find his way to the gangs and hook adolescent gang members and con them into doing volunteer interviews and then go back to the university. But that's a politically and personally dangerous way to do fieldwork research. I'm a university professor spending federal grant dollars. Those expenditures require me to abide by federal rules and regulations and are overseen by university administrative personnel and federal agencies. I had to abide by federal regulations pertaining to research data collection and privacy and confidentiality of subjects, and I also had to satisfy data collection requirements specified in the research design. The community's elected officials and agency administrators had to be made aware of the research and agree to collaborate; because Champaign's agencies were not recipients of federal grant support, their directors' collaboration was voluntary. I had to explain the project to the mayor, the school district superintendent, and the police chief and hope that they would approve of the project and agree to provide relevant data, and then I had to find my way into a local neighborhood where there were adolescent gangs. A wrong step along that chain of elected officials, agency personnel, and community citizens could easily have turned my assigned tasks into a nightmarish tangle of angry local officials voicing complaints to Spergel's office or the Office of Juvenile Justice and Delinquency Prevention.

Police see street researchers as a pain in the neck.[7] Police regard them even more negatively if they think that a street researcher facilitates, engages in, or covers up illegal activities (and thereby interferes with police investigations). Police commonly urge street researchers to stay off the street for their own safety. That warning means "Go away or get arrested if we see you within reach of illegal drugs." If I ignore the street police, the police chief gets angry. If a police chief gets angry and complains to city leaders who supported the project, I alienate those city leaders. If I lose the cooperation of the city leaders and therefore can't weasel the data that Spergel needs out of agencies, he gets annoyed. And if he gets angry, I lose his support and his grant dollars. A loss of grant dollars means the university gets angry. Or, worse yet, if police believe I have a role in drug selling, I'll be arrested and Spergel will either kick me off the project or more likely, knowing him, congratulate me on my enthusiastic style of gang research. When university professors get arrested for hanging around gangs and places where illegal drugs are sold, university administrators are publicly embarrassed, and universities typically do not willingly bail professors out of jail. I could weather an eruption by a chairman, a dean, or a provost, but firestorms involving police, local politics, and the criminal justice system are on an order of magnitude I couldn't handle alone. Self-interest in preserving my university salary, with its occasional hikes, kept me cautious.

Helping Hands

When the time came to get down to business and start collecting data, I had to solve two problems. First, Spergel's project required police and school data. I knew that marching into the office of the chief of police and the school superintendent and asking them to help out on the Spergel project wouldn't work. Cops and schools are leery of strangers. I thought the mayor might be the right place to solve my first problem. A solution to the second problem, finding and interviewing gang members, would come later.

The Champaign mayor welcomed me. I explained the research project. He didn't look too interested. I filibustered. I'm a cultural anthropologist, I said, just to keep the conversation going long enough to find an angle he'd support. The word "anthropologist" got his attention. The well-known cultural anthropologist Oscar Lewis, a faculty member in the anthropology department at the University of Illinois at Urbana-Champaign, and his family had been the mayor's neighbors decades earlier.[8] I told the mayor that my mentor studied under Lewis. Our common ground, a shared social tie to Oscar Lewis, sealed the deal.

I verified my identity and role in the project with official documentation. Mr. Mayor prepared a letter of introduction. He spoke to the chiefs of police and the school districts on my behalf. When I visited those offices, agency heads gave their support to the project without hesitation. No one asked about payment. The Champaign-Urbana communities were remarkably generous and welcomed the research project. Next, I needed someone to find gang members.

Headhunter

I was hired to do interviews. My clients were adolescent gang members. I needed someone who was a headhunter, someone who knew the streets and could be a legitimate guide. In Seattle, Popcorn, a local gang member and drug dealer well known to the police, took me places I couldn't go without him.[9] In Kansas City, Wendy and Cara, both members of the Fremont Hustlers, let me hang around, ask questions, and watch and listen. A legitimate guide does not mean a guy with street credentials, or "creds." Criminals know other criminals can't be trusted. Trust on the street doesn't come with committing a crime, getting arrested, being indicted, and being imprisoned. A legitimate intermediary means a local person who has earned a reputation by helping people, by, for example, aiding men fresh out of prison who are jobless, homeless, and friendless. A legitimate intermediary must be trusted by neighborhood citizens and the police, as well as gang members and street hustlers. A legitimate guide has to know that an outsider, like me, won't rip off people. Ripping off local folks in this context does not mean stealing property or snitching on them to police. An intermediary must sense that a researcher won't betray the faith folks come to place in his or her honesty and integrity.

Experienced street researchers know street kids don't trust adults. Street researchers must keep their word even if street kids don't. Trust must be earned. Trust means showing respect for the people we study. Respect means a researcher honors the trust kids extend to him or her when they agree to be interviewed.

Out of the blue I got a break.

The TV Panel

The local paper published a front-page article about the Spergel project. I wasn't happy to see my name next to the word "gang." Just the word strikes terror in the hearts of tax-paying citizens. No one I talked with at places like coffee shops, taverns, the cigar store, or the gymnastics facility ever mentioned gangs. That didn't mean there weren't gangs. How awful it would be, I thought, if I brought bad news to town, if champagne turned to vinegar on my watch, if I shattered a utopian picture of a college town in cornfields with the image of thousands of gang members lurking within a handful of first downs from Green Street.

I was fortunate. The article didn't cause consternation among local folks or lead them to make complaints. Citizens didn't call Illinois's senators on Capitol Hill with requests to solve the Champaign gang problem. The university's television station got wind of the news about gangs. A producer called me. I agreed to participate in a panel discussion on gang intervention and prevention. The producer said he had invited two additional panelists. That worried me. Local gang experts don't appreciate an outsider spouting opinions about gangs in their town.

Early on a weekday evening I drove the same fifty-five-mile route I had driven hundreds of times. I knew my way to the gymnastic facility. I knew how to walk from there to coffee shops and libraries. The campus was a maze of narrow streets. Getting lost was my forte. I drove around blocks, up and down Green Street, until I spotted a campus map at a sheltered bus spot. A quick look, a few twists here, a couple of turns there, and I finally arrived at the broadcast studio.

I felt nervous and timid. I was embarrassed to be Spergel's emissary on his project. He was one of three university researchers at that time who had studied youth gangs for more than fifty years. I was a novice. Honestly, I was at bottom uncertain of the ins and outs of his project. If I didn't fully understand Spergel's project neither would the audience.

I walked in and introduced myself to the first official-looking person I met. He shuttled me along to the producer, the fellow who called and invited me to the panel. He introduced me to the other panelists. One guy was a local activist. He seemed friendly. I was introduced to the second panelist. "Pastor Burpee, meet Dr. Fleisher." I knew I was in trouble.

Pastor Burpee was bone thin, about five-six, had a few days of beard growth, long before a few days' growth was trendy. His garb arrested me: a loosely fitting, light gray Nehru shirt buttoned to the top complemented by a white clerical collar and baggy gray slacks and gray alligator shoes. If the pastor's eyes could have shot bullets, I would have died on the spot. He hated me. I felt his animosity. I infringed on his territory. I threatened to block the sunshine falling only on him.

The moderator introduced panel members to the television audience. I was the professor, a gang expert. I felt Pastor Burpee's hostility intensify. I wanted to disappear. I read his thoughts. *This white man's a college professor. He don' know nothing about gangs.* I don't consider myself a gang expert. I am an ethnographer. I study a local culture's inhabitants. It doesn't matter if they are youth gangs, homeless ex-convicts, Mexican peasants, American Indians, Moroccan gangs, Turkish migrants, or federal prison inmates.

I hadn't met too many real-life ordained pastors. I'd known my share of self-anointed street hustlers and prison inmates who called themselves pastors or bishops. That gray garb with a white collar affords hustlers protective coloration, which gives them an edge when they're trying to scam citizens.

I decided that Pastor Burpee would be my headhunter. What's the worst that might happen? He could say no. I knew better. His hustle was money. My hustle was giving away cash to get interviews. "Dubs" (in this instance, $20 bills) would unite Burpee and me in a common cause.

Thankfully, the panel ended. I hesitated at first, then walked slowly and tentatively to greet the pastor. He feigned anger, projected hostility. I told him I'm an amateur, that he's the gang expert. He relaxed, a bit.

Pastor Burpee

He called himself Pastor Burpee. His friends called him Burp. Burpee's biography reads like a fanciful yarn a middle-aged criminal would spin to entertain listeners.[10] Over the first months of our acquaintanceship I learned the details of his life, from his birth to his sixth prison release. Thickened scars marred the backs of his hands, his knuckles. Heroin tracks, healed abscesses, scarred his forearms. Burpee knows hustling.

After the TV panel, our first contact occurred in the downtown office of the Champaign Prison Ministries. I walked in. Burpee was cleaning up ceiling tiles that lay in puddles left by a broken pipe. I told him what I needed. I talked about money. We planned to meet next at his new office in a small town north of Champaign at the site of a new Prison Ministries prerelease site. He chuckled when I called the prerelease site Homey Hills.

Homey Hills was a run-down, 1960s-era motel donated to Prison Ministries and paid for with private donations from local church members. The donations came after Pastor Burpee encouraged them to aid the forgotten men newly released from prison. He hustled building suppliers and tradesmen, convincing them that the sweat and labor they contributed to the remodeling of a run-down motel office and its shabby rooms was a blessing.

After a rocky start, our relationship improved, and Burpee relaxed in my company as we spent more time together on my research projects. The friendship pump was primed with cash payments to secure interview subjects, male adolescents who were self-proclaimed members of one of the north end's youth gangs. As the years passed, Burpee confided in me about local crime. He told me who was selling drugs, how drugs came into Champaign from parts unknown, and which of the many innocent-looking folks, like local ministers, were deep into the dope trade.

Burpee brokered my entrée into the north end community. I appeared on the north end tightly clutching a thick roll of dubs in anticipation of satisfying my data collection requirements for Spergel's gang intervention and prevention project. Burpee's headhunting expertise and hustling skills paid me dividends. Burpee knew gang members and where they hung out, and gang members either knew him personally or knew of him. They trusted him, and because they trusted him, they extended their trust to me. I interviewed hundreds of gang members, and several of those interviews opened the door to the Washington family.

Working the Streets

When I hired him, Burpee said I had purchased his protection services in addition to his assistance in locating gang members. I gladly accepted his protection, although I wasn't in physical danger. When his role as my protector became public news, our relationship gave me credibility as a white man folks could trust.

Late in the evening and into the early morning hours on Friday and Saturday nights and especially on what is referred to as Mother's Day, the streets were busier than usual.[11] I had a wad of dubs folded neatly and tucked down into a front pocket along with my driver's license, which was my identification on the few occasions local police stopped me, asking why I was hanging around a place where drugs were sold or standing on a street corner chatting with ex-cons known to the police. After I had a few conversations with local police chiefs, the word spread to undercover and beat cops that a researcher hung out at places where drug sellers satisfied their need for cash while drug buyers satisfied their need for chemically induced inner calm.

The search for gang members seemed never ending. I issued Burpee instructions, telling him, for example, that the following weekend I would need to interview twenty-five male gang members, no younger than seventeen, who were on probation. Burpee screened interviewee candidates, culling those who didn't meet interview criteria, such as having a verifiable gang affiliation or a history of probation or parole. He rounded up the gang members in a large van and dropped them at interview locations. Finding one hundred gang members, screening them, and then driving them to interview locations like somebody's house or garage or backyard required months of effort. The way Burpee located gang members remained a mystery. I teased him, asking if he used a gang member divining rod. He would not tell me where he found them. Best I could get was "I know people." If he told me where he found gang members, I could find them myself. He'd lose money.

Interviews were conducted close to home, in gang teenagers' neighborhoods. When it was necessary, I paid to rent interview space in private homes, and in order to get paid, a head of household had to meet specific conditions. I explained that I must conform to federal privacy regulations when conducting interviews. I didn't want anyone listening to interviews from around a corner in the kitchen or the top of the staircase in a duplex apartment. Occasionally I had to rent bathroom space, sit on a toilet, and use a hamper as a desk in order to ensure privacy.

Burpee called beforehand to tell me the addresses of interview sites. Interviews, to which I brought students who wanted to learn how to conduct interviews, proceeded over long hours, often from early afternoon into the mid- to late evening. A good number of the criminal justice undergraduate and graduate student interviewers were residents of Chicago's least desirable neighborhoods. On occasion, an interviewer and an interviewee had attended a Chicago high school together and then went in quite different directions. Some of my interviewers, men and women, ran the streets in their younger days. That instant mutual identification between a current gang member interviewee and a former gang member cum college student interviewer inevitably increased interview time. Longer interviews generated more data, and the return on investment of money and time grew. A few student interviewers had more criminal history than some of the gang members they interviewed. My college interviewers, I am glad to say, landed on the optimistic side of the proverbial desk.

Hustling Interviews

The interview requirement of the Spergel project took years to complete. Burpee hustled volunteers. I paid them. I was conducting other research studies on the north end at the same time, for which I required interviews with adults, including parolees, probationers, gangsters, and thugs on the run.[12] I had hundreds of hours of interviewing to complete and couldn't wait for a magical moment when a sense of rapport washed over informants to carry out the interviews. Awaiting rapport wastes time, money, and reduces the return on investment. Criminals don't stand still. I had no assurance that the men I wanted to interview would be on the street in an hour let alone days or weeks later when I got a clue that rapport was imminent.

Street research falls prey to people's dislike of a researcher who barges into their neighborhood, gets too pushy, and feigns camaraderie to cajole an interview, only to then disappear and never be seen again. Overcoming the animosity folks feel toward a researcher who playacts rapport and then fades away cannot be resolved with cash. The reverse situation occurs too, when hustlers playact rapport with researchers and exploit them for cash to gain the momentary glamour of the interview spotlight.

Days of driving around with Burpee, talking to local civilians and street folks was a test. He tested my style of interaction with locals. Was I able to talk plainly to local folks face-to-face without sounding like his idea of the way a college professor talks? I understood his motive. He didn't want me to embarrass him. I didn't want to embarrass myself. If local folks didn't respond well to me, Burpee might lose a modicum of the community's trust. If that happened, I would have been on my own, hustling my own interviews. I passed Burpee's test. If I hadn't passed, it's doubtful I would have completed in a timely manner the hundreds of interviews the project required.

Fieldwork is a mutual hustle. Potential informants have an advantage. They have what I need. They don't need me. It's a sadly mistaken researcher who thinks the homeless, ex-cons, addicts, drug dealers, and gangsters proffer personal experiences only because researchers are good folks who need their help. Moreover, scholarship suffers when a street researcher loses his or her professional identity.[13] It's easy to get lost on the street, lose track of your research mission, and succumb to a misbelief that you (a researcher) play your street role well enough to blend in on the street and assimilate to the role of a street hustler or a gang member and become one of them, even for a day. Equally delusory is the belief that a street researcher can be a savior, pulling folks off the street, altering their life path, helping them become more like us.

Dubs, the $20 bills, were the quintessential payment. I had teenagers refuse to do an interview for $10. "Gimme a dub or I walk," they'd say. I can't recall how many times a teenager asked for a loan. "Mark, you got some I can hold?" "Some" referred to a dub, and "hold" meant "give me money," in the sense that a parent gives a son or daughter an allowance. If a teenager gets one dub, he or she figures there are more dubs he or she can con me out of. It's none of my business what a teenager or an adult does with his or her dubs. Dubs buy weed or condoms or Doritos or sugary soda or ice cream or diapers or groceries. What they buy doesn't concern me.[14] I don't know any college professors who refuse to pay his or her daughter an allowance, thinking he or she will buy weed. I didn't see the harm in handing a gang member a dub in exchange for an interview. That exchange of a dub for information might be one of the few nice things an adult has ever done for an adolescent. Acts of kindness come without strings attached. The nauseating cliché "teach them to fish" might work with well-fed teenagers and adults. Hungry people need dubs to buy food.

Fieldwork over months or years requires a continuous stream of non-monetary exchanges more personal than handing a teenager a dub. Exchange has many forms. I offered gang members advice on ways to interact with police and how to talk to teachers in a manner that didn't get them suspended or expelled.[15] I drove teenagers to hospitals to visit sick relatives. I babysat for a mom who had gone shopping and expected me to sell dime bags of weed to customers knocking on her kitchen door. I paid with rides around the neighborhood. I bought lunches and dinners at Pizza Hut and fast-food joints. I accompanied people to visit friends in the local jail. I pumped up someone's jail commissary account.[16] The single most significant long-lasting payment offered in exchange for the right to walk around someone else's neighborhood where you don't belong takes the form of a kind word, a smile, or the patience to listen to (not interview) teenagers and adults who never had a chance to talk to a white man who wasn't arresting or prosecuting them.

Spergel's research staff designed an extensive and detailed interview protocol that I used in more than four hundred interviews. My fingers ached after I filled in blank lines and checked boxes on more than fifty pages for each interview. Spergel received the data he paid for. His return on investment was high, and he was satisfied. I wasn't. After doing at least four hundred interviews, I knew little more about the lives of youthful gang members and their community than I learned from responses to interview questions. "Yes, I live with my mother." "Yes, she has been in jail." "Yes, she drinks alcohol and smokes weed." "Yes, I don't know my father."

Structured interviews generate mounds of data in the form of snippets of information. In order make sense out of those snippets, I needed to get knee-deep in the north end's day-to-day hustle and bustle, watch life acted out, listen to people talk about their lives, and hear the tales of happenings on north end community.[17] I wanted to understand the nature of the shared knowledge that shapes the north end's culture and social reality.

2

Culture and Social Life

The north end was a quiet, low-income residential neighborhood during the years I was there. No homeless folks panhandled by day and slept by night on sidewalks or under bushes. No bag ladies pushed swiped grocery carts packed with heaps of plastic bags. Street corners didn't harbor drug sellers, and local gang youth didn't hold court there or in parks.

North end social life had sights and sounds common to families in neighborhoods around Champaign. Parks and playgrounds enticed youngsters to find amusement on grassy fields on sunny days. Hanging out and sharing gossip with friends on a midweek afternoon in a park sustained friendships. Warm spring afternoons when the sun was high and the air warm, I enjoyed seeing young mothers like Melody and her gramma strolling on the sidewalk and pushing a baby carriage, a simple act that symbolically solidified the fragile kin ties linking past to present to future generations. In another place, later in the day, Vonda invited Melody and her friends to attend a birthday party for Gina's six-year-old daughter that was being held at Vonda's Section 8 house.

Learning Culture through Folklore

Spoken words, the things people say or sing, are folklore.[1] Folklore expresses a culture's collective understandings, which are embedded in a community's culture.[2] Things people say aren't necessarily facts, and there are no objective standards by which to measure the accuracy or veracity of what people say to interviewers or one another.[3] Rulers are objective measures of distance. Thermometers measure temperature. We can measure distances in miles, yards, feet, and inches between Bloomington and Champaign. We can measure Champaign's temperature on January 1, 2001, in degrees, either Celsius or Fahrenheit. People don't voice objective opinions. Assessing the accuracy, the veracity, of things people say, interpreting what people say within the context of a culture, poses challenges more complex than reporting a number on a ruler.

Ethnographic field research collects a chronicle of verbal accounts and observations of behavior. These verbal accounts are stories composed of memories, the incidents people have seen, heard about, or participated in. Memories are idiosyncratic recollections that can be influenced by a person's personality, mental state, and biases, as well as their verbal skills that portray the intricacies of stories. Stories can be as simple as recounting what people have said about one another. They can be as fresh as the report of a theft that occurred five minutes ago or as old as the recollection of an event a month or a year ago. I heard people tell stories about what their friends did or should have done, or what their friends didn't do and why they didn't. I heard stories told in the first person about incidents on the north end long before the storytellers were born.

Over time, as stories are told and retold, storytellers revise gossip, rumors, anecdotes, and hearsay by amending the characters, storyline, action, and finale. No matter who's telling the stories and how often these are repeated, stories transmit cultural knowledge, attitudes, beliefs, and rules of behavior, person to person, one generation to the next. North end stories were a compendium of cultural guidelines for prescribed and proscribed behavior.[4] A unique feature of north end stories was an absence of moral and ethical judgment. North end stories didn't chastise pregnant fifteen-year-old girls, nor did stories harshly criticize adolescents who dropped out of school. Pregnant teenagers and school dropouts weren't scorned, belittled, or alienated. Their mothers didn't scream insults at them. Families weren't distressed or embarrassed. Men and women arrested, convicted, and imprisoned weren't alienated or degraded because of their criminal conviction, nor did north end folks act suspiciously or shadily when they returned to the neighborhood from prison.

North end culture didn't pass moral judgments on sexually active teenagers, teenage mothers, convicted felons, or biological fathers who simply walked away from their social parental duties. The moral connotations of political expressions such as "single-parent house," "teenage pregnancy," "below the poverty level," or "absentee fathers" are culture-bound and were not part of the natural speech of north end residents.[5] North end culture prescribes personal responsibility. It expects community members to handle the consequences of their behavior without laying the undue burden of those consequences on family and friends.

Community, Memories, and Relations

North end culture has captured and defined the collective memory of black migrants who moved to Champaign from Tennessee, Kentucky, and states in the Deep South over many decades. These black migrants brought with them a dedication to hard work, an embrace of tolerance, and a willingness to blend into a dominantly white community.[6] Migrants who settled the north end shared common sociocultural adaptations to conditions of slavery in southern states. The descendants of former slaves came north possessing a shared culture and a worldview geared toward fostering and protecting interpersonal relationships.[7]

Black and white communities coexist in an amicable relationship, side by side in Champaign-Urbana, separate and equal by virtue of historical events that neither side controlled.[8] White and black culture and social practices are different and equally legitimate within their own cultural communities.[9] Rich or poor, it's comfortable to be among people who share your language, culture, and understanding of the world. The north end community was not an economically and a socially degenerate neighborhood where blacks resided by default owing to white flight. Communal life on the north end represents a black culture that possesses a unique history, folklore, and standards of prescriptive and proscriptive behavior. Black culture emerged as a byproduct of centuries of hostile interaction between whites and blacks. The north end community's cultural beliefs, values, and social rules are outcomes of centuries of black culture's adaptations to privation in a segregated America.

The north end's social reality and oral history are a negotiation, a consensus among neighbors who share lore and debate its merits within the limits of each person's idiosyncratic memory bank.[10] Personal and community memories are a cultural bank account of tales of relationships, which convey guidelines to personal interactions. Community lore portrays acceptable patterns of community life. Memories of interpersonal reliability or untrustworthiness, insults, tragic personal events, and accounts of mutually beneficial relationships are the currency of north end social life. Currency increases in value in a neighborhood where people see each other often and rely on the quality of mutually beneficial relationships. Memories, rumors, and gossip travel over social distances at a remarkable speed from person to person in the north end's informal communication network.

Relationships of trust and interpersonal reliability are conveyed to listeners when Niece tells her friends Joyce and LaShanda that Sharon assisted Kendra by babysitting her two young children. These accounts of interactions are memories people share about one another. Collective memories guide social life. Today's gossip about Yvette insulting Joyce, a love affair between Mickey and Shanice, an impending fight between Butch and Donald over Donald's romantic intentions toward Butch's girlfriend are fodder for memories. True or false, exaggerated or accurate, as long as these bits of folklore stay active, these tales create social reality.

Living Black portrays the north end neighborhood community's way of life. This depiction, which is based on what I saw and on what people said, reveals social structures, social patterns of interaction, and functions of social interactions. Observations and verbal statements were the basis of my searching for common ways people think about, describe, and explain the behavior of people around them. These shared, common ways of thought represent a neighborhood community's worldview.

Oral History and Lore

By 1904, the north end was a small well-established black community.[11] Census records indicate black migration to Champaign from the Deep

South and surroundings states occurred predominantly after 1910.[12] Over the decades of in-migration, black migrant settlements straddled the Illinois Central Railroad, linking Chicago to southern states and traversing the northwest corner of Champaign. The Cleveland, Cincinnati, Chicago (CCC) and St. Louis Railway traveled east-west, linking cities across central Illinois. Black settlements along the north-south Illinois railroad and north of the CCC and St. Louis railroad grew into a section of Champaign referred to as the north end of the track.[13] The Illinois railroad divided the north end into an east and a west side of the tracks.[14] On the east side were black public housing projects. By the 1990s, only a single housing project, the Pines, remained occupied, all the rest had been closed. South of the Pines was a neighborhood of single-family residences that extended a few hundred yards toward the northern edge of downtown businesses. On the west side of the tracks there were single-family residences that housed up to three generations of family members in a single house.

The collective memories of the elder generations of the north end regarding its founding are integral to its oral history. Elders' tales convey the culture of the north end's community life, a culture of self-sufficiency that endorses values of cooperation and mutual alliances that depends on patterns of kinship and friendship.[15] Elders' spoken narratives outline the prescriptive and proscriptive behavior necessary to achieve and maintain social order. These elders, the great- and great-great-grandparents of today's families, preserve memories of their grandparents.[16] Their memories tell of their ancestors' northward train migration in the late nineteenth and early twentieth centuries to Chicago, responding to the call for workers advertised in northern cities' newspapers. Trains stopped to disgorge passengers at Champaign. Folks who couldn't read well mistook the "Ch" in "Champaign" for the "Ch" in "Chicago," or so the story goes. They disembarked. The north end population increased and housing expanded as more black migrants chose to get off the train, where they met their friends and relatives and, elders said, reunited with family from their birthplaces in the South. The north end grew out of family and friendship networks. When I arrived, social life still rested on a framework of friendship and kinship relations.

Black migrants settled in the midst of a community that offered jobs in domestic employment in the homes of university faculty, in fraternity and sorority houses, and in the food service industry. Segregation generally kept blacks and whites apart in their neighborhoods, yet blacks were employed and had stable households.[17] The social link between the north end and Chicago was solidified by firm segregation and Chicago's harsh treatment of both black migrants and northern-born blacks.[18] Blacks fled to Chicago suburbs and rural Champaign to escape the racial segregation of Chicago, its menial jobs, and its often violent treatment at the hands of whites.[19] Around that time, so the story goes, the north end acquired the moniker Little Chicago.

Elders and late middle-age folks share memories of the north end at a time of peace and tranquility, when early generations of working parents bought houses while children attended segregated schools. Then at some unspecified time, something disturbed the peace. That period seems to have been the racial unrest of the 1960s and 1970s. Race riots broke out in Detroit and Cleveland. Violence erupted. People residing outside the north end described the neighborhood as wildly dangerous, festering with gangsters, and inhospitable to outsiders. Black north end residents don't share that view.

Stories from that period of racial unrest labeled the north end a dangerous neighborhood. A few cops told me that patrols feared sniper attacks and hesitated to drive through Little Chicago in the 1970s. A retired white teacher said that when she visited students and their families on the north end in those years she was not permitted to drive on the streets; she had to park outside the north end and be escorted by a north end resident to students' homes. By the time I arrived, the north end's reputed dangerousness had become symbolized by and embedded in Little Chicago stories. Local folks told me that outsiders were still fearful of being victimized and avoided driving through Little Chicago. University faculty I knew ashamedly admitted they took shortcuts on north end streets to the interstate, sliding up windows, locking doors. Folks can't be too careful in black neighborhoods. Friends told one of the white graduate research assistants who worked with me on the north end that she and her girlfriends should avoid the area. If they got lost at night and found themselves there, friends advised them to drive through red lights and escape the neighborhood as quickly as possible. Rumor had it that coeds would be dragged out of their car and victimized by young black men. When that white research assistant accompanied me to the north end the first time, she hesitated to leave the car. Prodding helped. I assured her she was safe. She mustered up her courage, opened the car door, and huddled against the car. Soon she was hanging out, laughing with the fellas, and doing interviews with male and female gang members. The north end community's black oral history doesn't contain tales of a segregationist, racist white community or tales of the black community fearing attacks by whites.

Media stories preserved and disseminated Little Chicago's reputation. The blocks of shabby houses and decades-old, dilapidated public housing projects—combined with impressions created by watching black gangster movies, listening to news descriptions of drugs and gang shootings in nearby Chicago, and reading eye-catching headlines about the prevalence of blacks in prison—might well have led whites to conclude that north end blacks were like those they heard about in the news and watched in movies: dangerous and violent.

If you drive through the community without foreknowledge of tales of its dangerousness, all you see is a small neighborhood of old wooden houses, old and rusty cars jacked up along sidewalks, broken concrete streets, potholes large enough to swallow a VW Beetle, and black kids walking to hoop at the park, young mothers accompanied by their aunties and grammas strolling along, pushing baby carriages. The north end did have its share of gun-toting crazies and fools wielding chains and baseball bats. I saw them. There were a few. When the crazies and fools put down their chains and bats, though, even they were civil and friendly folk.

Told and retold, north end residents' memories are a continuous source of debate and humor. Through this sharing process, historical accounts are revised and community folklore is reshaped and blended with local neighborhood culture. Local oral history and folklore include a compendium of people, places, events, stories of race relations, histories of family lineages, and tales of amicable and hostile relations between and among families that broadcast community values, beliefs, and morals in a public forum. Telling and retelling tales of times long gone creates folkloric accounts of personal experiences from a time that no one recalls that lacks historical details.[20] The north end I spent years getting to know was a community with two faces.

Inside the North End Looking Out

North end folks had only a slight interest in local, regional, and national politics. Only a few voted, read newspapers, watched television news, or had friends outside the north end.[21] As far as they could tell, the outside world showed little political interest in the north end's citizens.[22]

Low income on the north end has been the norm since the 1930s.[23] Low income has shaped social interactions like tracks shape train travel. A few more dollars now and then helps buy diapers, pay a few bills. Selling dubs (in this instance, $20 bags of weed) at home carries little risk. A young mother can sell five dubs five times per week and garner more tax-free cash than minimum-wage workers earn in seven days. Selling dubs doesn't require bussing to grocery stores to mop and sweep floors or to restaurants to wash dishes and haul garbage cans. Working at home doesn't require bus commutes ninety minutes one way to a mall across town.

Low income on the north end has created an egalitarian community. No one covets thy neighbors' property. No one begrudges thy neighbors' lifestyle. No one plans spring break or Christmas skiing vacations at Aspen. No one covets Tanisha's beat-up, rusty car. No one has a gold or platinum card. There are no identity thefts. No high-interest debt. No high mortgage payments. No exorbitant rents. No foreclosures. No payday loans. Life with less money shapes patterns of social interaction among kin and friends, and it plays a role in the decisions that folks make about the products that they buy.

Life with less shapes patterns of social interaction. Relationships acquire value. Who you know, how much you enjoy the companionship of kin and friends, and how much you trust them alter patterns of social interaction. A person's social wealth is not measured in the economics of net worth; rather, it is measured in the number and strength of social ties to friends and family.[24] Friendships, kinship relations, trust, and reliability are the coin of the realm.[25]

Social attachments are a form of credit cards and savings accounts. Attachments extend all the way across the distances between residences that separate friends and family in the north end. Missie's "people" are those who ascribe momentary and long-term value to exchange relationships. Some friends and family buy her baby's food or diapers. Others share their food. Social attachments have short- and long-term value. Girls who hung out together on the street at age fifteen rely on one another at age nineteen when they're mothers.

Relationships with men come with a high cost. Young men sap the value out of women's relationships with other women. When Missie's baby's daddy Brandon dumps her in exchange for her friend Yvette, both women lose a friendship. Lost friendships equal lost social resources. Lost friends mean fewer people to babysit or share food. Lost friends mean fewer people to call if you're evicted and need a place to stay. Social security on the north end depends on durable, trustworthy friendships, which over time shape a culture of mutual cooperation.

The geographic distance separating friends and kin relationships has long marked the geographic limit of the north end's young women's willingness to venture outside their homes. Young women only traveled as far from home as their most distant friend lived, a pattern well established in the 1930s.[26] Champaign's agencies offered employment training that north end folk chose to disregard. To gamble homeland social security in exchange for more income was a high-risk bet, fraught with few assured rewards. North end folks find social security among kith and kin in relationships that have lifelong benefits. It felt good stay home and close to friends and relatives.

Local Assets

Public transportation extends north and west across the interstate, carting passengers to shopping malls, chain restaurants, and motels. The journey from the north end to employment venues across the interstate highway took ninety minutes, with timely connections. Bus-stop enclosures south of the Pines keep rain off newly coiffed hair, and in the dead of winter, the wind blasts icy particles that feel like bees stinging frozen skin. Bus tokens, folks told me, cost about a buck each way. On an average weekly $250 income, daily bus travel cost a north end worker at least one hour's worth of post-tax income. Child care expenses gobbled up more net income. Friends helped out, now and again. Young women without children did not offer to help out with daily child care obligations unless they were paid. Dubs were always acceptable payments.

Women with children supported one another. Teresa, an unemployed woman in her mid-thirties with two children, lived rent free at the Pines. Her friends needed child care. Teresa agreed to watch their children. Her friends' children played with her kids. She said an extra few dollars would help out. Word got around. Teresa soon had kids running everywhere. Day care, she was pleased to say, gave her a worthwhile task to do and helped her friends. Women who couldn't find a reasonably priced babysitter quit their jobs. Teresa, an honest soul, reported her modest babysitting income to the housing authority and soon received shocking news. Her monthly rent increased to $500. Teresa faced a damned-if-you-do, damned-if-you-don't catch-22. Undisclosed income would lead to eviction, a bad thing; helping her working friends, on the other hand, was a good thing. Teresa stopped babysitting.

The north end had no child care facilities. Young mothers who needed help finding child care, or help paying for it, did not reach out to local agencies. Nike, fifteen years old, said that when teachers at her public school learned she was pregnant, they were extremely solicitous. "I had social workers crawling all over to help," she said. However, she added, "When I had my son, they disappeared." She quit school. Girls who remain in school become pregnant more often than similarly aged girls who drop out.

A three-store strip mall on Fourth Street, three blocks south of Bradley Avenue, was the north end's sole source of potential employment.[27] A Korean-owned convenience store that the kids called the "Koreans'" store or the "nigga sto" sold takeout fried food. There was also a beauty salon and a store that sold candy, chips, and ice cream. These stores, locals said, were not owned by north end residents. They did not employ local folks. There were no black-owned businesses on the north end.

There were no bars, clubs, liquor stores, or convenience stores selling alcohol on the north end or within easy walking distance. The nearest grocery stories were downtown, too far to walk with children in tow while lugging grocery bags. Cheap motels near the north end offered the only source of low-income work within walking distance, where women worked housekeeping jobs. If they hired on a full-time basis, hourly wages were higher than what you would earn for part-time work. Some women worked a full-time job a few months, quit when making beds and cleaning toilets became intolerable, and took another full-time job when necessary. Housekeeping wages, part-time or full-time, often were supplemented. Guests' electronics, watches, cameras, and whatever else these girls pilfered were handed over to the Fence, a local fella, who had a street version of an import-export business.

Farther away, northwest across the interstate, there were restaurants and mega grocery stores. A few teenagers I knew worked as cashiers in these large supermarkets. They giggled as they told me it was a good thing the cash registers did the math. They couldn't subtract well enough to make change. A few stole cash out of the registers and quit before management caught on and called the cops.

3

Lively Streets

According to Burpee, in black neighborhoods, "Life happens in the street," for all to see. Cars stop in the middle of the street. Friends hang out of car windows, smoke cigarettes, and chat like they are parked in an empty lot.

On a warm evening, Sylvia strolled along a sidewalk south of the Pines. She saw me wandering around, waved, and beckoned me. I walked across the street to meet her, she walked toward me, and we met in the middle of the street. She was delighted to tell me that she had just enrolled in a vocational education program. Cars swerved around us. No horns. No one yelled. Life happens on the street. North end streets were portrayed in distinctly different ways in local folklore.

Two Faces

The north end had two faces, one soft and welcoming, the other hardened, portending the area as a dangerous place. The north end I saw in the 1990s was a peaceful, sleepy enclave of black and white neighbors. The north end I heard about was an angry, gang-ridden, segregated community. In the 1930s, "To many of the residents of the two towns [Champaign-Urbana], and especially among the policemen, this [black] section is known as the 'Jungle.'"[1] Sixty years later in the mid-1990s, I walked along north end sidewalks accompanied by a Champaign police officer assigned to handle gang issues, in addition to his primary duties.[2] He said that the north end harbored more than four thousand gang members, that the police database did not distinguish between gang and nongang offenses, and that gangs were no longer a serious crime problem.[3]

I watched white and black police officers on patrol stop to ask ex-cons if they were doing okay, if they had jobs. Chuck, Jaboo, and Crazy Eye and I hung out near dusk. A few blocks away, Chuck spotted an unmarked patrol cruising nearby. He turned toward me, reached into the back right pocket of his filthy jeans, "hold this." He handed me a box cutter he used on the job at a warehouse. "If they find this on me, I'm going back to prison." The patrol car slowed; a barely visible wave could be seen through its darkened windows as the police passed us by.

Folklore set in the 1970s told a tale about gangs on the north end different from folklore set in the 1990s. The officer said that back in the 1970s there were "real" gangs roving the north end, unlike the current gangs in mid-1990s, whose members comingled, walking around together side by side. Vice Lords and Gangster Disciples, the officer said, were then the major gangs in the 1970s, and they had hypervigilant members who hunted out rival gang members. Real gangs, he said, warred over selling drugs and ownership of home turf. Real gangs hated the police, sniped patrol cars.[4] Back in the day, real gangs controlled the north end. Outsiders, a paraphrase for whites, were required to gain permission from local gang members even to walk on north end turf. A school administrator told me that he needed a black escort to accompany him on visits to students' families on the north end.

My research assistants and I interviewed hundreds of adolescents who asserted gang membership to satisfy the requirements of the Spergel project. I interviewed dozens of adult men, like Burpee and Alabama, who asserted a Vice Lords and Gangster Disciples affiliation, on a study funded by the U.S. Census Bureau.[5] If real gangs were only those committing serious crimes and whose members fought one another, the Champaign police were correct. There were no real gangs. I didn't see gang turf. There were no warring gangs. Gang members I knew never had the zeal to snipe at police. Police patrol officers stopped and yakked, and laughed with adults and adolescents in conversations about school, jobs, and life in general.

Police said gangs were not a problem; there were no gangs on the north end. Yet north end residents, men and women from their twenties to sixties, avowed membership, predominantly in the Vice Lords and Gangster Disciples, although these gangs had no visible reality in social and economic life in the mid-1990s. Folks who claimed gang membership didn't huddle and plan drug sales or associate in single gang-dominated groups. No one even hinted at abiding by orders barked by gangs' top dogs. No one bragged about being a gang leader; no one pointed at someone, saying he or she was the gang leader. There was no gang graffiti. Adolescents didn't partition themselves in cohorts wearing blue or red or black. There were no gangs of adolescents huddled on darkened street corners in the wee hours of morning. No one said they needed to rush off, to attend a gang meeting.

Burpee, a self-proclaimed Black Gangster Disciple, had friends who were Vice Lords, Gangster Disciples, Mickey Cobras, and Black P-Stones. He said, "The streets aren't like they used to be." I couldn't verify or dismiss his or police claims of back-in-the-day gangs, nor would I summarily accept his and police claims of a once violent gang reality.

People learn by listening to things other people say. In that sense, until proven otherwise, gangs were not a social reality like the gangs reported in the 1970s. Still, the verbal reality of the gangs from the 1970s festered in the mid-1990s as police folklore on community gangs. Folklore embeds kernels of lost historical reality transformed into cultural beliefs. Folklore records memories, remnants of historical events. Police culture's gang folklore, I presumed, was likely grounded in the racial discord and hostility between blacks and law enforcement in Chicago, Detroit, and Cleveland in the 1960s and 1970s. Chicago was the fourth most segregated city in the country in the 1940s; violence against blacks was prevalent and well documented.[6] The ongoing black migration from Chicago and Detroit to Champaign was a likely source of rich tales of violent gangs that diffused by moving from big cities to rural Champaign. These accounts might have affected the community lore regarding the relationship between the Jungle's black gangs and the cops, introducing an element of hostility.[7] Gang violence, a proxy of inter- and intraracial violence, was solidly lodged in local folklore, even if gang violence didn't occur in Champaign.[8]

By 1999 I had been working on the north end for about four years as Spergel's researcher when he came to Champaign for the first and only time. I told the police chief that Spergel wished to express his appreciation firsthand for the police chief's years of assistance on his project. We met in the chief's conference room. I introduced Spergel to the chief and senior police personnel, and he thanked the officers for their assistance and asked about the local gang problem. Police personnel thought a moment, silently nodded in agreement, and said there were no gangs on local streets. Professor Spergel and I politely slipped away.

Hustles

A hustle gets a guy what he needs with the least effort and the highest return on investment. My hustle was doing research interviews. Hustling offers a way of life, off the record, a lifestyle that doesn't require paying taxes.

Most north end folks labor hard at honest jobs, but some prefer to hustle. Some work all day and hustle at night. Some work a while and then hustle a while and then work again. Buster, a work-site laborer, sweated all day, at minimum wage. Thin paychecks didn't cover household bills. Selling dubs of weed some evenings paid the bills. The best hustles don't end in arrest. On the north end workers and hustlers coexisted without cause for alarm.

Burpee worked two straight jobs. Prison Ministries satisfied his ministerial needs; his monetary needs were met by managing a boiler room, a call center where men and women made outbound cold calls selling all manner of questionable products. He trained and supervised dozens of folks. Many were ex-cons. Cold callers nestled in cubicles, pitched their goods, all day, every day. The boiler room conjured an office climate reminiscent of a prison dayroom, where these hustlers cum inmates had played cards, chess, and checkers and watched television. In the boiler room, they read scripts, trying to sell car insurance along with whatever other products they were told to pitch. That boiler room suited ex-cons. Conning folks out of money exploits hustlers' best skills. If only customers knew they were volunteering personal information to sales people who just finished sixty months in prison for embezzlement, robbery, or being a felon in possession of a weapon.

It's hard to hustle full time.[9] It takes training. A hustler-to-be needs a mentor. There's a lot to learn. It takes time, effort. It's trial and error. Journeymen like Jaboo, Alabama, Crazy Eye, and Burpee mastered the streets early on. They learned street culture. They knew where to go on the streets. They knew how to avoid trouble. They knew who was dangerous. They knew where to hang out, where they'd sleep, where they'd get fed. They knew they'd eventually get hauled off to prison. The hustle-jail-prison cycle is part of street culture. Hustling skills are honed on cell blocks, in jail dormitories. Released, hustlers know how to get back in a hustle on the street.

Men like Burpee say they're "from the street," were "raised up on the street," "went to the street," are "going into the street," have been "on the street," and "know people who lived and died on the street." Burpee was a lifelong denizen of the streets. He lived off the record, off the books. He was invisible. The street doesn't refer to a place, a sidewalk, a corner, a housing project. The street refers to a way of life. The guys sleeping in doorways or near heat vents in the sidewalk, the guys that citizens walk by and pretend not to see, they're on the streets. The street is a metaphor, a way of talking about a person who hasn't had social stability, social support, or opportunities to find legit employment. Guys who were raised up on the street don't know how to live anywhere else, nor do they want to. That they have been "on the street" means hustlers share a way of thinking about their personal history and lifestyle. A street lifestyle doesn't have prerequisites. There are no background checks or drug tests. No résumé is needed. No diploma required. People go to the streets when high school's zero tolerance policies expel them, when they are trying to escape the grasp of a sexually predacious stepfather, or when they believe they don't have "people" who will worry about them on cold, dark nights when gun shots resonate among houses on the block. The street connotes a social space that's timeless, endless, absent of direction.

Even though the north end's young women weren't raised up on the streets, they knew how to hustle.[10] It's just one of those things kids learn by osmosis on the north end streets; they learn how to survive on the fewest resources. The north end's teenage mothers complement government benefits with on-again, off-again, small-scale sale of weed in ten-dollar ("dime") and twenty-dollar ("dub") bags. Pregnant young women may sell dimes or dubs steadily over a two- to three-week period in order to earn enough cash to buy baby clothes, diapers, or a crib. If their government benefits stopped, these young women would know how to work a hustle.

Growing up, many of these young women had a stable home life, stayed with family members surrounded by friends. Their grandparents owned houses passed down from their great-grandparents. Their grandparents had legit jobs. Their moms worked legit jobs or stayed at home, raising young children. The girls who called themselves gang members were legitimate members of the north end community. They were today's generation of skilled survivors.

Folks raised up on the streets prefer hustling over straight jobs, even if jobs are available to ex-cons, many of whom are victims of high school expulsion and are semiliterate. Straight jobs are tough. Jobs require structure and take too much time. Supervisors lurk. Good hustles allow men and women freedom. In his younger days Burpee ran a slick drug hustle. He employed "shorties" (minors) as runners and street-corner sellers. Shorties' hustle was risky, although there were always available apprentices, school dropouts, teens whose drugged parents didn't care where they were, and teens running away, escaping violent homes. Burpee expected to do time. He planned for it, when he was "slinging" drugs. "Ya gotta plan on it. Treat shorties good and when I come back to the street they're going to run the drug hustle on this corner. They give me action."

Being on the street doesn't require committing crime. Street culture rejects no one. The homeless, the injured, the uneducated, the emotionally damaged, the cognitively impaired, the neglected, the abused, the rejected, and the expelled are all welcome.

Wooch, in his mid-teens, was raised up on the street. "You're never alone if you're into crime and learning how to do crime," he explained.

"We [kids on the street] don't think about what's going to happen. It's all about the money. In a group you have more eyes [but] doing crime in a group makes it harder to get away [with crime]. I do what I do with guys I been knowing a long time. I trust'm. It's hard to leave crime. Them boys don't see the advantage in working or taking an education." Being on the street wasn't his choice. Wooch went to the street as an orphan at age ten. His mother "got religion," he said, and threatened to tell police about his father's lucrative hustle. His father hired a contract killer. Wooch's mother was killed. When his father went to prison, sentenced to life without parole, Wooch got life on the streets.

Spots

Tourists ride buses around the nation's capital. Guides identify the Lincoln Memorial, recount stories about slavery and freedom. Places like those have meaning imbued with emotional content. The north end is a living historical memorial commemorating black migration to a safe place.

There are places where social things happen, places with significance in local culture. If you hang around the north end long enough, you'll hear people talk about where things happen. Notable places are called "spots." Drug spots are common. "My spot" refers to one's residence. The term "spot," used instead of "house" or "apartment" or an "address," has connotations in north end culture. People move, a lot. Taz stayed at Corleone's spot. Diedre stays at Myeshia's spot. No one knows the mailing address of Shanice's spot, like no one knows Nike's given name, Iresha's neighbor at the Pines. But not everywhere is a spot. Kids' playgrounds are playgrounds, not kids' play spots. Places where buses pick up passengers are bus stops, not bus spots. The place where kids go after school to buy Doritos, candy, and soda is a convenience store, not a junk food spot.

Street corners, driveways, and bits of property acquire personal qualities in the stories people tell about their community. These stories, exaggerated, twisted, or apocryphal, become the evidence that supports folkloric themes in the community's oral history. Burpee and I drove around the neighborhood in his aging Cadillac, stopped at street corners, in front of houses, pulled into church parking lots, drove by empty fields. He showed me spots, slivers of the neighborhood history. Burpee animated spots, voicing street-life themes in north end folklore, police arrests, back-in-the-day shootings, drug busts, and residences of the north end's legendary crime families.

North end spots serve as guideposts, points of social interaction where players hang out, where social life happens. Burpee showed me spots. Folklore transformed those places into sources of the history of local social life.

Players

People rise and shine and go off to work. Every few weeks, paychecks arrive. Free of the anxiety that hustling engenders, these folks settle down, live a quiet life. They pay taxes. They abide by the rules of their community. They are civilians.

Inveterate street hustlers are players. "Streets are tough, prison's easy," Burpee declared, citing the players' maxim.[11] Players vacation in prison, he said, like he had done most of his life. When we worked together even he abided by rules, except for paying taxes, because he thought it ridiculous that his tax dollars were used to pay for prisoner confinement. In the course of his life, he had been a player, a con man, a drug seller, a strong-arm thug, a recidivist, a guy who'd rather work around the rules than abide by the rules. He'd been a hustler, a player in the game of street life. He'd been a thug who couldn't envisage a citizen lifestyle.

I puzzled over why Burpee, unlike Cliff, Tracy, and Stump, quit selling drugs, stopped gangbanging, and gave up strong-arming weak people. He was a journeyman criminal and proud of his toughness. He flourished in prison, which was just another place where he plied his criminal trade. On his sixth prison release, though, something happened.

Newly released ex-cons search out a hustle, even though prisons offer inmates education and job training. In jail, prisoners had opportunities to acquire job skills with economic value or finish a GED. Illinois prisons were rife with inmate programs; landscape architecture, carpentry, and even optometry programs were open to inmates who demonstrated a modicum of self-control, avoided the appearance of gangbanging, stopped fighting, quit assaulting staff, and attended ninety days of GED classes.[12] Inmate players choose to hustle and violate prison rules and regulations, even though they knew they'd get busted; they can't hide in prison. Inmate hustlers sell cigarettes and illegal drugs and hustle commissary scams for their own immediate benefit.[13]

It's easy to spot newly released ex-cons wandering on the north end's narrow streets. These men are clothed in prison-issued boots and blue-denim pants, and sport prison-made polychromatic tattoo sleeves. They don't walk like citizens, who stride along with a purpose, shout at passersby, or turn to scrutinize the rear end of a woman who just walked by. New-to-the-street ex-cons adopt protective coloration. They try to project an appearance of strength; instead, they meander. No place to go. They're friendless, jobless, helpless, and exude hopelessness. Their faces are blank, flat and emotionless like a sheet of plywood. Their eyes see but don't register the predicament they're in. They're strangers in a familiar land, a land to which they never belonged.

When Alabama hit the street, twenty years older than the day he walked into the penitentiary, he wore invisible armor, and his squinty eyes signaled distrust of everyone. Anticipating an aggressive move by anyone who came near him had produced creases on his forehead that sent a clear message: "Don't you dare fuck with me." Alabama made it safely to Burpee's door.

Ex-cons like Alabama were disarmed by Burpee's demeanor. He knew how they felt. He had had lots of practice. Most released prisoners had never had a permanent, safe place to stay, and they don't have one once they are back on the streets. Silently, they wish they could stay in a safe place near people like themselves, preferably not a religious mission, where homeless men and ex-cons are forced to endure sixty minutes of religious chatter before they're fed.

Burpee understood the trauma that ensues when inmates are released to the streets. He knew what released inmates need. He knew what they wanted. They wanted to be cared for. They wanted food, recreation, companionship, a safe place to sleep. The streets don't accommodate those longings.

Ex-cons need an extensive, structured adjustment period, especially after spending twenty years in prison like Alabama had. Released inmates had to cram legit survival skills, which they hadn't acquired before they were locked up, into the early weeks of a stress-filled return to the streets. After their adjustment period, which Burpee helped them manage, he set up ex-cons in jobs that matched their skill level and personal propensities. Alabama's ass-kicking skills were outstanding. Burpee set up a job that required just that skill set.

Cliff meandered. We met across the tracks, on the west side. I didn't know him. We approached each other. I nodded, said "Hi." He stood in front of me. I stopped. He thought I was a social worker. "I need a job," he uttered, his voice marked by a southern drawl. The way he said "I need a job" wasn't a request. It was a plea, a cry to help him.

Cliff grew up in Houston, Texas. He did time in Texas "camps" (prisons), before wanderings with a profit motive pushed him toward Illinois. There, offering inexplicable reasons, he says, "I just got caught up." Busted, imprisoned on drug charges, Cliff met Bruce, a fellow convict, at Pontiac, an Illinois state penitentiary. Bruce offered him his assistance after his release. He told Cliff to wander to Champaign's north end and look him up when he got there. Cliff's gullibility floored me. I kept my opinion to myself. That Cliff believed Bruce awaited his arrival attested to Bruce's acumen as a hustler and illustrated how Cliff's naiveté got him caught up. Cliff was lost, in all senses of the word. No friends. No cash. No job. No place to stay.

Cliff wasn't forced to sleep on the street, behind dumpsters, in early winter's icy wind. I gave him options, including a religious shelter or a public mission. Those, however, were both definite no-no's. He could have checked in at Prison Ministries. He didn't. Two and a half years in a crowded penitentiary cell block changes a man's concept of desirable sleeping arrangements.

I felt bad. Cliff didn't seem like a bad guy. A drug beef was not a big deal. I didn't see neo-Nazi tattoos splayed across his neck or teardrop tats down his cheek or an FTW (fuck the warden) tat on the back of a hand or "love" and "hate" inked on his fingers. A lack of prison ink revealed a touch of character.

Soon Cliff had a new acquaintance, Tracy. An inveterate crack addict, a multiple recidivist who was newly released, she was his sole ray of hope, a truly depressing thought. Tracy stayed at her sister Patti's drug spot. Patti refused Cliff accommodations. Still homeless, Cliff rambled on city streets, ran a panhandle hustle downtown, hooked up with Jimmy, an ex-con road dog. Cliff and Jimmy tucked in behind dumpsters at the rear of an eatery on Green Street. Didn't take too long before cops rousted them.

Tracy eventually had enough of Patti's nagging her about abiding by parole conditions, like kicking the crack pipe and trying to find a job. Bearing those burdens of a straight life was too much stress for Tracy. Mind you, this wasn't the first time Patti had tried to keep Tracy straight. She'd been in and out of juvenile confinement and jails and prisons since her teenage years. Patti kicked Tracy out, back to the street. There's Tracy. No job, no plan, no money, and a major drug habit demanding satisfaction.

Cliff and Tracy knocked on doors looking to find a warm, dry spot, in early winter, and eventually they found one. They shacked up in a garage tucked away behind a ramshackle house, which, except for the barking dog on the front lawn, looked abandoned. Barking dogs on front lawns are a stranger alert mechanism, announcing the arrival of drug customers or cops. I spotted Cliff and Tracy wandering about a few times over the next months. They decided to use their best skill set. Selling drugs worked well until Cliff got fed up with Tracy. "Had enough of her shit," Patti said when Cliff beat Tracy up. Back inside to the safety of warm cell blocks. Street's tough, prison's easy.

Paroled, Again

Burpee described three types of ex-convicts on north end's streets. The first type of ex-convict includes men and women who find themselves in trouble. Cliff was released from a Texas prison, then somehow "just got caught up" in crime that landed him in an Illinois prison. Men like

Cliff could have quit crime and walked away, Burpee said. "They didn't. They were stupid."

The second type of ex-convict includes addicts whose crime supports their addiction. Tracy said that if she had to do prison time in order to smoke cocaine rock, it was okay by her. Crazy Eye, a rock cocaine and heroin addict, had been busted repeatedly for committing strong-arm street robberies, stealing jewelry and wallets, pawning whatever he could, selling stolen credit cards. Violence generated cash that fueled his addiction, rock by rock, injection by injection. Burpee said he strong-armed Crazy Eye, calmed him down, got him a job, and helped him kick the buzz of robbery and hard drugs. Blunts and "forties," forty-ounce bottles of fortified malt alcohol, helped take the edge off.

While I was ambling around the neighborhood in early afternoon on a warm spring day on my regular walkabout to see who was hanging out, I met a white woman strolling on the sidewalk in front of me near Patti's. She looked lost. I thought if she came by that spot to get high, she was in the right place. If she was hooking, she was in the wrong place. Hookers didn't hustle the north end streets.

That forlorn-looking white woman, about my height, five-seven, with light brown curly shoulder length hair, had no visible tattoos on her forearms and neck. "Love" and "Hate" weren't tattooed on the top-side of her fingers. She didn't wear prison-made black boots or prison blues or browns, the attire of those released from state and federal prisons. Her clothing and hair didn't issue a nasty bouquet of stale cigarettes or weed smoke.

Wendy, the white woman, stopped in front of me. "You a social worker?," she asked. I explained who I was and what I was doing on the north end. "I need a job, can you help me?" I didn't know the local job market, I explained, although there was a guy who might help her. I gave her directions to the Prison Ministries office downtown and suggested she talk to Burpee.

Wendy told me a familiar tale. She'd been imprisoned on a drug beef to support a drug habit more than five years ago. She did her time, was released and got a job, and worked diligently and maintained a modicum of straight lifestyle. Then a background check by her employer picked up her criminal history. She had been fired recently.

"What did you do? What was your job?" I inquired about her lost job. I thought if she worked in an office handling paperwork with people's names and addresses and social security numbers a company might not trust her with that sensitive personal data. Dismissal on a felony conviction in that job would be justifiable.

"I untwist tassels," she said timidly, "you know the tassels that hang on graduation caps." Tassels are twisted into knots, threads may be missing or damaged in odd ways. All day, every day she untwisted or repaired tassels and attached that tiny metal band that keeps tassels neat, tidy, and hanging properly.

"So you untwisted tassels. That's it? No office work?"

"That's it. All day I untwist twisted tassels. I got fired. I have a prison record. I been working [there] the last two years untwisting tassels."

Wendy lost her job. She lost her apartment. That day was the last time I saw her in the neighborhood. She couldn't be trusted to untwist tassels.

The third type of ex-convict includes hard-core career criminals. Burpee said guys like him thrive on gangbanging, the buzz of criminal activity, and the pleasure of overpowering the weak. Burpee said these types of guys won't stop running the streets; they'll do whatever they want, no matter what threats and punishments the courts hold in store. They'll stop hustling and hurting people when they decide to quit or get killed on the streets or when they are threatened by even tougher bullies on the streets or inside cell blocks.

Young women are vulnerable to physical and sexual exploitation if they are not protected by aggressive brothers or cousins or female friends willing to pick up baseball bats, chains, or a pistol to protect them.[14]

Stump, an ex-convict from Chicago in his mid-twenties whose prison cellie stayed on the north end, arrived on the streets near the Pines. Physically fit, muscles developed on weight piles in four Illinois prisons, Stump caught Kesha's attention. In her late teens, Kesha was single, had no children, and ran the streets, free and easy. A few blunts later, their sexual relationship was off and running.

Kesha felt affection, which Stump perceived as vulnerability, a young woman easily manipulated. Stump's affection had a price. Stump bullied Kesha into selling drugs. If she refused, she caught a beating.

Kesha sold dubs. Tasha, Kesha's mid-teen sister, attracted Stump's attention. He'd double his income if Tasha joined Kesha selling drugs. Kesha's hesitation bought her a whupping. Tasha sold drugs. Stump bullied her into sex. Stump's cellie lurked in the background, reinforcing threats of violence and rape. Stump and his cellie threatened the sisters when they tried their best to escape from drug selling and victimization. Squealing begets a beating. Luckily, the Pines had ears and eyes. The sisters' cousins picked up the news about Kesha's and Tasha's beatings. Word got to Stump and his cellie that the girls' cousins were gunning for them, and they disappeared quickly. Stump carried to the street the aggressive and violent exploitation of the weak witnessed in high-security prisons.

Newcomers

North end was a residentially stable area and had been over generations, according to local elders. Families at the Pines raised their children there. Across the tracks to the west, single family houses that lined the blocks had been occupied for generations. I knew of one three-generation family that had lived under the same roof since gramma, the elder member of the family, inherited it from her parents. On occasion a front yard displayed a For Sale sign. I didn't see families move out of or into houses in the neighborhood, or commercial movers hauling furniture into or out of houses, or local folks with rental trucks moving place to place. Slowly people slipped unobtrusively into the stable population and spread out into nearby neighborhoods. Those folks relied on street trades like selling drugs. Some came there to hide out. Wandering into the neighborhood without a local connection to a friend, family member, or former cellmate can leave a male wayfarer without a place to stay, except for the nearby men's mission. There weren't abandoned, boarded-up drug houses or foreclosures newcomers might use as a squat, and even if there were squats, neighbors didn't put up with squatters and other types of freeloaders.[15] Kin folk and friends of friends continuously flowed in, arriving unannounced one day from unknown places, blending in like they'd been there all along, and then one day, without notice, they were gone.

Young women migrants in their late teens and early twenties said Chicago's neighborhoods were stressful. They needed to "get a break" from "the streets." A close look at these female migrants showed they were episodically homeless transients. They weren't welcomed with open arms and had to rely on the largesse of friends and relatives or else bed local guys in exchange for a place to stay and food.

Household composition from day to day was unpredictable.[16] Beds were limited. Lack of sleeping space challenged women with multiple children who were staying in one-bedroom apartments or small Section 8 houses. The lady of the house occupied the single bedroom. More sleeping space became available like space at a campground. Single mattresses were squeezed into corners and along walls in hallways. Couches turned into sleeping spaces, offered on a first come, first serve basis. Floor space, a pillow, a thin blanket was a guest suite. When big sister or brother was carted off to prison, it came as welcome relief to Junior, who'd been sleeping on the floor or couch or sharing a twin bed with a few siblings. When an older sibling came back home, Junior got the floor again.

There was often trouble when imprisoned relatives returned home. If relatives wouldn't take a released convict back in, his next best chances were his baby mamas' places, where he stayed until the first, then second, then third baby mama kicked him out. By the time she booted him out of her home, an ex-convict baby daddy had eaten her food, smoked her weed, and most likely impregnated her again. If he hung around a few weeks, his baby mama knew cops would come banging at her door and arrest her baby daddy for dealing drugs, fencing stolen property, assault, weapons possession, or violating parole by failing too many mandatory drug tests, if he showed up to take required drug tests. More than likely he'd be arrested for domestic violence and hauled back to prison. Then his baby mama relaxed.

Kirk, Bailey, and Baker were out-of-towners. They showed up to hide out. A prison partner allowed them to say with him as long as they supported themselves. It wasn't too long before they moved on to sponge off of a girlfriend of their prison partner's girlfriend. They hung around a few days, then disappeared as quickly as they appeared.

When Mario was released from prison, he didn't bother looking for a job. He mooched off his grandmother. In the company of several prison partners staying nearby, they huddled up most afternoons and enjoyed a weed smoke-athon.

Javon mooched off his gramma. She didn't know he was hiding out. Had she known, she would have kicked him out before police arrested him, which caused her to be evicted from public housing. Javon said he was on the run. Gang trouble in Los Angeles pushed him east, he told me. Champaign was a long way to go to hide out. I didn't think Javon could locate Los Angeles on a map. Javon couldn't describe details of his cross-country trek. He couldn't remember if he took a train or bus or hitchhiked. He lied about residing in Los Angeles. I knew he was lying when he said he'd never heard of the famous Pink's hot dog stand.

Danathe, a transient in his early twenties, showed up one day. He said he was from Danville, a town to the east of Champaign. He appeared on the streets on a Friday in the midafternoon at a sidewalk drug-selling spot. He said he had no friends or relatives or girlfriends on the north end. Strangers don't drop in like skydivers. He left soon after he showed up.

Anthony, Robert, and Nat "came up together," they said, in the same neighborhood. They gangbanged at an undisclosed location, too secret to reveal. They were stealthy dudes. They didn't know anyone on north end streets, they said. They didn't have local acquaintances they'd met in jail or prison. Their plan was to rent a house, sell drugs. Outsiders don't just appear and set up a drug business. If they did intend to sell drugs, they'd need a friend or relative or they'd have to know folks on the street. They, like Danathe, quickly disappeared.

A bus delivered Alabama. He met Pastor Burpee when he had ministered to his imprisoned flock. Alabama paroled when he completed every day of a twenty-year sentence at the Stateville prison in Joliet, Illinois, and several other state prisons. Scenes from the movie *Natural Born Killers* were filmed at Stateville.[17] This prison was known for its roundhouse, an early twentieth-century multitier, circular brick and mortar cell house.

I met a young man, early twenties that I'll call Stranger. Stranger had his name scrawled across the left side of his neck. His forearms displayed geometric figures, a crown and what looked like a Jewish star. Stranger had a cousin at the Pines. People I knew at the Pines knew his cousin.

Stranger said he had fled Chicago just in time. He had escaped a gang-inflicted punishment called a violation while working for Smooth's drug business. When Stranger failed to give Smooth all the cash he'd garnered in drug selling, he got a serious violation. Stranger faced a medieval-style punishment he described this way. Fellow gangsters would dump him on his back on a makeshift table, in someone's garage or an abandoned building. His extended arms would be yanked downward toward the floor. His legs secured at the thigh, his lower legs would be bent at the knee, and pulled toward the floor. There, helplessly secured on his back, Smooth would beat Stranger's chest and stomach with a baseball bat. The number of wallops, Stranger said, depended on the amount and number of times he had allegedly withheld cash. That violation was not Stranger's first offense. Death was the ultimate penalty once a violation was averted, he said. Sounded to me like an apocryphal tale. Even so, groupthink was sufficiently pathological to conjure a frightening degree of sadistic thought.

Spot, Players, and Fieldwork

Learning the rules of local street culture had to be my first step. I had to learn where to find informants, where informants were most likely to be hanging out midweek at three in the afternoon or at six in the evening on Friday. On the first day of my research on the north end, I started a walkabout. Walking, biking, or slowly driving around at different times on weekdays and weekends allowed me and neighborhood folks to see one another. Local curiosity eventually gave way, and my method paid off. Folks approached me, asking what I was up to. Their inquisitiveness opened the door. Done regularly, walkabouts reap benefits. Chatting up locals eventually unveils the neighborhood's social order, the way invisible ink gradually appears under ultraviolet light. When people know you, they appear out of the shadows.

Conducting interviews, making observations, and hanging out at spots require a lot of time. Players come and go, bouncing like stainless steel balls in a pinball machine. Bouncing players have a social order, though this social order operates on rules different from mine. The trick is to recognize that players don't bounce capriciously, nor do they stop at random places. Players bounce in specific directions, crisscrossing one another, creating networks of social movement. Unless you know the flow of players between spots, players just seem to disappear quietly into a neighborhood's social haze. Players hide in plain sight at spots where they know people. Cops know that too, but players are aware in turn that police departments aren't funded well enough to hunt them down if they're wanted merely on misdemeanor or nonviolent felony warrants.[18]

My sense of time and personal responsibility is different from that of players. Players don't wear watches. I didn't know anyone who did. I didn't see kitchen clocks. Adolescents coming up on the streets, ex-cons on parole, and hustlers disregard court orders. The idea of appearing in a specific courtroom at a specific time has no meaning in street culture. Folks on the street know that failure to appear in court always results in an arrest warrant. They fail to appear anyway. Parolees and probationers violate terms of release, even knowing full well they'll be arrested and hauled back to prison. Ex-con players can't meet simple reporting requirements. I kept reminding myself that ex-cons were once adolescents on the street who didn't attend school at all or else were suspended and expelled from school.

I needed to know the people who were well known by a lot of people. I needed to know where they went and with whom and why they went to particular spots. The trick was to tease out the social structure that creates patterns of interaction.

4

Everyday Life

Pine Village sheltered families in decent family housing, nothing fancy.[1] Work crews in winter shoveled deep snow, pushing it to the edge of parking lots and along sidewalks, where it piled up into high mounds. When snow smelted, work crews wielding spears impaled gum wrappers, empty cigarette packs, soda cans; others raked leaves, fixed repairable fences. Workers seemed to enjoy raking dust off dirt, fertilizing bare ground, and pushing power mowers over grass-free lawns. It was an admirable effort. Children slid and swung and climbed on new playground equipment erected at the front entrance. Mothers chatted. No signs warned drug sellers that enhanced drug-selling penalties would be imposed on anyone who was foolish enough to pitch dubs near that playground and got busted for it.

Burpee escorted me to the Pines on a windy, chilly day in early fall, on my first visit to the complex, for what was to be my initial meeting with the Washington family. He parked his blue Caddy on a six-car parking lot close to the rows of apartments on the Pines' west side. That parking lot eased mothers' schlepping of groceries on one arm, kids on another.

Burpee, wearing light green slacks, a greenish shirt, green alligator loafers, and a gold cross that hung halfway down his chest, skipped along ahead of me on the cracked walkway. He stopped about halfway.

He pointed down, to his left, to the spot where Big C died. He ordered me not to speak, to let him do the talking, at our destination, the Washingtons' apartment at the west end of the ground-floor, two-story apartments at the back of the Pines.

Swirling wind whipped the screen door, causing it to bounce off the door jamb on the Washingtons' front entry. Drawn window shades blocked my view into the apartment. A ripped bed sheet, pinned to a wall above narrow windows on each side of the door, blocked my view of activity inside. The television blasted through the walls like solar wind.

Burpee's familiar knock sent an unambiguous message that it was a friend who was visiting. His knock didn't silence the clamor inside. Knowing how to knock reminded me of a secret society. Knocks weren't as silly as three knocks fast, two knocks slow, then two knocks fast. Close, though. Friends' knocks are unaggressive. Not too hard, not too loud. Cops' knocks are forceful, aggressive, loud and hard. Cops' thunderous knocks create instantaneous silence. Calvin, one of the Washingtons' sons, taught me how to knock like a friend. It took a while. I needed practice. Eventually I learned the friend knock. Still, years later, after I had earned the right to walk freely into the Washingtons' abode, as close friends did, I couldn't resist a cop knock. In my mind, I still hear Calvin's voice saying, "Mark, don' knock like you a cop. That scary, man."

I pinned the swinging screen door, quieting it against the jamb. Door banging was a no-brainer fix, like other things I saw that needed fixing. A graduate school professor told me that a cultural anthropologist can learn to live anywhere, deserts to jungles, with space technology or stone tools. His remark was intended to bolster my courage and keep my enthusiasm up when I was about to be dropped in a settlement of cactus-walled huts in the Mesquital Valley, a desert in central Mexico, a place where summer heat could melt rubber. The Pines was a far better place.

Poor folks share that same we-can-live-anywhere attitude by necessity, not by design. Theirs was not a domestic culture that invested time and energy in fixing noises that would've driven me crazy. Banging doors and squeaking rusted metal on flimsy screen doors merely blended into lively noises of kids laughing inside.

Inside, I stood timidly near at the entrance. Moving into family space without an invitation seemed inappropriate. But then I decided to meander about anyway.

The living room, fifteen to twenty feet long and twelve feet wide, had windows on the exterior wall facing south that gave a view of a space between apartment rows that turned green in the spring. The interior north wall opened into a narrow rectangular kitchen, the same length as the living room, with enough space to allow two people, maybe three if they were small, to pass each other without turning sideways. A sixteen-step carpeted staircase in the living room led up to three bedrooms and a bathroom.

The Washingtons' back door faced north and exited the kitchen, opening onto a narrow patch of overgrown weeds bunched against a rusty east-west fence line encircled by brambles and thorny greenery. Beyond lay acres of unused land, cleared and leveled. That flat, barren zone reminded me of forests' firebreaks, or the vegetation-free zone that encircles penitentiaries, a zone rifle marksmen rely on to get the best aim at a proverbial five ring on the back of an escaping convict.

A baseball bat was propped against the vertical door jamb of the kitchen door, within easy reach, and on the floor and pitched upward against the jamb was a butcher knife resting on its wooden handle, large enough to use like a machete. Families without a baseball bat handy used a defensive object like a heavy link chain positioned on the floor against the wall and hidden from outside view behind a fully opened door. One end of the chain was wrapped with tape and provided a better grip.

A quick escape route, the back door, leads to safety if an unwanted visitor throws the front screen door open, runs in wielding a handgun, looking for an intended victim. That happened, once, on the west side of the tracks. A teenage girl, well liked and well known on the north end, sat alone on her couch watching television on a midwinter night. Her ex-boyfriend, crazed by jealously at the thought of her new beau, burst through the front door and shot her several times in the abdomen. He ran away. Friends of the murdered girl knew the shooter. They guessed he hid in his friends' apartment nearby. People hide with people they know. If friends knew where he hid, cops knew too. They nabbed him before he caught his breath.

Set back in an alcove in a kitchen corner, a washer and a drier eased laundry chores, although the heat that escaped around the edges of worn-out heavy rubber gaskets prevented the drier from staying warm enough to dry wet clothes. The drier's incessant rattling churned luke-warm air, hour by hour, day by day, summer through winter. An endless flow of heat over hot and humid summer months escalated indoor temperatures to the point that they matched the swelter I recalled from the Suffern (New York) High School wrestling room. High heat in summer, the endless blasting television, kids' noises, and the constant door slamming explained why in places like the Pines, Burpee said, black folks hang out on stoops.

The living room overflowed with young teenage girls and a few teen boys, huddled together, sunk into an overstuffed beige, three-cushion couch. They were giggling, unable to stop staring at the oddity, a white bald guy standing next to Burpee in the Washingtons' apartment. The kids' stares didn't obviously say "Hey, look, a white man," but it was close. One of the couch girls barked, "Ma, somebody's here." That was Iresha. In her new sneakers and basketball shorts hanging to her knees, Iresha looked like a bright, energetic middle-school student. Her eyes sparkled. ReRe, her family nickname, was pronounced "re" as in *key*. She and I chatted. She had a dream: to receive a scholarship from the University of Michigan to play on the Wolverines women's basketball team.

Public housing and a need for food stamps don't trap children in places like the Pines, I thought, restraining them and keeping their dreams at a distance. ReRe just might get to Ann Arbor. At that moment in the living room, I didn't know that I'd hang around long enough to watch the hopefulness and happiness fade, that Iresha's path would be filled with insurmountable obstacles. Reality overpowers dreams in places like the Pines.

Iresha's sister LaWanda, a few years older, stared at Burpee and me. Bennie and Willie, the youngest sons, scurried, waved, smiled, unfazed by our visit. Handsome young fellas. Nice boys. Jason, the eldest Washington son, a few years older than Big C would have been, was not there; he was doing his third term in state prison at age twenty-seven.

My attention was drawn away from the noisy teenagers and toward a woman, who was sauntering toward Burpee and me. Dressed in baggy light brown pants and a billowy shirt, her face projected suspicion tinged with hostility. About five eight and stocky, Maureen, known as Mo, looked at Burpee and me. Before she asked too many questions, Burpee spewed his rap. "Mo, dis here da white man, white man wid da money." As Mo heard the word "money," she perked up like a hungry lion spotting a slow-moving antelope. As we chatted on, suspicion and hostility faded into a grin. Her eyes spun and came up double aces on a walking white slot machine. She stared at me. If I could have heard thoughts, I'd have heard her say: "I hit the jackpot."

Burpee referred to me as "da white man." I took "white man" to be a compliment, a sign that he recognized our differences and that our differences were okay, as long as I had a roll of twenties in a front pocket. Burpee's racial enlightenment hadn't yet emerged, but cash trumps racial intolerance.

I reached into my left front pocket, withdrew a folded roll of twenties. Mo's eyes opened wide, an unguarded smile creased her face. Her right arm stretched out to grab the roll. "How'd you get that money?" I explained—more like babbled—about the research. "Who da fuck would pay you to do that fo'?" Good question. I suspect taxpayers want to know, too. I wondered that myself. Money won out. Mo's question faded into the realm of rhetorical inquiry.

I let her know I needed a private, quiet place to do interviews and then explained interviewee compensation. At that point, I knew things would get sticky.

"Each interviewed kid gets a dub."

"A dub? You payin them little mudafuckers a dub! You'd better pay mama." She stuck her arm out, fingers on her right hand curled back and forth, like she impatiently awaited cash to drop out of an ATM.

"You in my house, now, white man wid da money. Dubs!" Her sarcasm tickled me. I knew we'd get along.

Burpee kept quiet, didn't intervene. I knew that when I told Mo about interview fees, she'd hammer me. That conversation with testy Mo was one of Burpee's many tests. He wanted to know how well I handled folks like Mo. Burpee's protection pay was considerably higher than hers.

As negotiations continued, Mo turned away, moseyed into the kitchen, left me standing, talking to the air. When she ambled back, she held her arm out again and curled her fingers back and forth. "Come on now, dubs." She reminded me, like I'd forgotten.

Walking away while someone spoke was not considered rude. Lots of folks did it. I thought what I had to say was important to her. Was I ever wrong.

Teenagers hanging around the living room pushed a wooden coffee table to the end of living room within a few feet of where I was doing my chitchat negotiation with Mo, until she wandered off, again. When she turned away, I looked down at the table. There I spotted two Illinois academic achievement reports, one for Iresha, the other for Bennie, the elder of the two youngest sons. Both scored well above the mean on reading. Bennie hit a few percentage points above the math mean. ReRe was a bit below the math mean, yet within easy reach. If she had a bit of tutoring, I thought, she'd be on course for the Wolverines women's basketball team. If ReRe could find her way over the hurdles that lay between middle school and high school graduation, she might succeed and make it to Ann Arbor.

Burpee got bored. He had a hard time just standing around doing nothing. He seemed to feel uncomfortable around those kids. If only Mo stood still long enough to finish our negotiation, we could get on with doing research with the kids in the living room. I indicated that I would pay each kid a dub. However, in addition, she wanted a dub per kid interviewed in her apartment for herself. I refused. Each kid, I explained, spends two hours answering questions. That much time deserves a dub, I responded, but not her rental of the space to me. She drove a hard deal, though, and eventually I agreed on a fair cash payment per kid, if she satisfied one strict condition. Payment depended on an interview space that was private and quiet, an ideal condition, often undoable in public housing. Privacy rules must prevail.

Apartments like Mo's were not ideal interview spaces. Interviewing in a living room or kitchen puts bystanders in earshot of responses. Kids hide to listen. Covert listeners who are silently taking pleasure in the question-answer repartee will reveal themselves. The kids unthinkingly jump into the conversation, offering their own take on a question or agree or not with an informant's answer. So few adults pay attention to what these kids say that they become excited when an adult listens to them. I did mock interviews in newly rented spaces to test the likelihood that covert listeners lurked around corners or in upstairs bedrooms. Covert listeners' eagerness to join an interview can become overwhelming quickly. On many days I wished that I had a portable interview space, like a "port-a-office," that I could pull behind my car and set up anywhere, anytime.

Burpee and I hung around Mo's apartment. Over an hour, our negotiation came to a slow end. Burpee declared to Mo within earshot of everyone in the room that he was my protector. That didn't surprise me. He protects me; he protects my dubs, his income. Still, whatever his reasons, I didn't think I needed protection, and his insistence on protecting me sucked the air out of my lungs. But maybe Burpee knew something I didn't. Maybe I did need protection. Then I thought back to our first conversation after the television panel. We met in his Prison Ministries office in downtown Champaign. He sat with his feet up on the desk, bottoms of his shoes facing me. "When I used to talk to white men, I sold them cocaine or insurance." That day, at Mo's, Burpee sold me insurance.

My introduction to the Washington family had long-term consequences. Years later, I hired Iresha and LaWanda as paid research assistants on a third research project.[2] The Washington girls had connections to dozens of teenagers and young adult friends who claimed to be gang members. It seemed every teenage girl on the street knew or knew of Iresha. She had dozens of male and female friends. ReRe was outgoing, had a sense of humor, loved to laugh, and had a ferocious temper she kept well hidden. Her friendliness attracted friends. Her aggressive nature kept friends close.

LaWanda, on the other hand, kept to herself. She was withdrawn and had a smaller social circle than Iresha, although they shared some friends. When LaWanda got pregnant with Mario's child, several years after we met, there was less contact between her and those friends who didn't have children. Girls without children continued to hang out a lot, smoke weed, gossip and giggle, and soon faded away. Even though LaWanda didn't smoke weed at all, her friends said she shouldn't be smoking weed now that she was pregnant. Teenage girls agreed that pregnant girls shouldn't hang out on the streets. They might get hurt. They needed to rest and stop hanging out at all hours of the night. LaWanda had many advisors. These teenaged girls told me they had health classes at school. They learned birth control methods, the danger of sexually transmitted diseases, methods of STD prevention, and self-care during pregnancy. Yet the mean age of first pregnancy was sixteen.[3]

Mo's Rep

The matriarch of the Pines lineage of the Washington family had a reputation. I stopped by their apartment a few days after I first met Mo. The living room was again filled with teenage girls, chatting and laughing. The television blasted noise high enough to cause hearing damage. Iresha greeted me. I asked, "Your mom here?" Memphis was sitting with friends at the kitchen table playing cards; he leaned back in his chair, mouthed the word "Hi," and waved his fingers at me. "She's on a mission," Iresha replied. "A what?" I asked. "A mission," she repeated. Memphis overheard my question and Iresha's answer, shrugged and turned back to his card game. Standing nearby Bennie and Willie chortled. Mo often disappeared without telling her kids where she was going, Iresha explained. "When she coming back?" Iresha shrugged and said her mom might be at her gramma's across town. It was her gramma's birthday.

Iresha and I drove across town to visit gramma, Mo's mother. We arrived at her gramma's well-appointed, factory-built home. A well-dressed late middle-aged lady with newly coiffed hair greeted me. She was entertaining friends, who ate small cookies and sipped tea out of china cups. When introductions all around ended, she inquired about my research. Iresha said I was a pretty nice guy for a teacher.

I smiled, nodded, and eventually got around to poking a few questions into the conversation among ladies playing gin rummy. The ladies laughed like drunken frat boys when I asked about Mo's missions. Gramma's stories about Mo running off on missions ever since she was a teenager kept guests entertained and startled no one. Gramma invited me back any time to join in card games. "You play cards?" I smiled, shook my head side to side. "Too bad," she said disappointedly. "We'd like to take your money in a poker game."

Mo's rep spilled over onto the white side of town. I went to a police station one morning to drop off boxes packed with documents saved from a past research project. Kathy, a civilian employee, allowed me to use the department's industrial paper shredder, a machine the size of an SUV. While the machine shredded paper files into fine strips, Kathy asked if I knew the Washingtons. No, I hadn't met them, I replied. Confidentiality about whom I'd met and what folks said were critical, particularly in a cop shop. She said the family was quite a bunch, a "handful," as she put it. If I met the family, I'd enjoy Mo, she commented.

Several decades ago, Kathy had worked in a school district office. Teenaged Mo raised hell in school. The police knew her well, too. She met Mo's mom at a school function. Kathy praised Mo's mom and said she worked hard and did her best to keep Mo straight. Kathy didn't mention Mo's siblings. I didn't ask. No reason to ask a nonfamily member kinship questions. Recollections of Mo's antics gave way to laughter among office folks seated near the shredder.

By the time I completed my research on the north end, Mo and I had become quite fond of each other. It didn't take effort to get Mo talking. She loved to talk. She was like a story jukebox. Put in a dub, she'd talk all day. Her gruff, domineering manner was a transparent facade. She howled at her older son one minute, then spoke softly to her young sons. In an instant, though, her smiles and laughter became annoyance. She'd get fed up with blasting television noises, kids running in and out of the broken screen door that would squeak and slam all afternoon into the evening on warm days. Mo had a talent for adding raucousness to mayhem, like the time shortly after we met when I watched her, kitchen knife raised high in her hand, chase Calvin, smiling and laughing, out of their Pines apartment and down the sidewalk close to the spot where Big C died.

Memphis and Mo

Memphis stood a lean six-feet tall; his body hunched ahead a few degrees as he walked, as if he carried a heavy load. He had a methodical gait, barely lifting his well-worn, ankle-high black boots off the ground. In threadbare jeans and one of his many colorful long-sleeve shirts often marred by a frayed collar, he spoke slowly, slurring his words, when he grew tired. Memphis had a long fuse, nonplussed by just about everything, including Mo's missions that lasted weeks at a time. He didn't get worked up when Mo set off on a mission or screamed at the kids or chased Calvin with a long kitchen knife. He had a talent I lacked. He found a quiet spot inside. Memphis withdrew to a peaceful place somewhere between a full-on encounter with the outer world and total withdrawal, a learned skill men acquired doing prison time.

Mo was a handful. Memphis balanced her craziness. They were kind to each other and found a place where each could live with the other. Mutual kindness extended to those times that tried parents' souls. Twon killed Big C only yards from the Washingtons' front door at the Pines. Jason had recently been sentenced to prison, again. Death and imprisonment, inevitabilities they took in stride. Mo erupted in anger but Memphis wasn't even fazed when Calvin's mate horsed around with a pistol and got the family evicted from the Pines. But neither was he flummoxed when the second-floor toilet dropped through the living room ceiling at their next home, the Blue House. They moved, again. They adjusted nicely to their relocation in one large room at a women's shelter. They weren't irritated at me when I meddled in family affairs and complained about Iresha's first boyfriend, that miserable weasel. They didn't shout angrily or say nasty things to each other. They endured heavy burdens well. Mo's missions were a therapeutic timeout, I guessed, that allowed the family calmer days and lowered the odds that Mo would add mayhem to raucousness.

Mourning

Soon after Burpee introduced me to Mo, our negotiation over the cost of renting space ended. Burpee had things to do, places to go, people to see. He disappeared. Mo and I stood together. I said nothing. I appreciated her cooperation. I wasn't about to grill her. Simple questions can be taken as interrogation. Timing is everything. She broke the ice.

She told me about Iresha's hoop skills and her dream of college basketball. She talked about their youngest sons and their success at school. She said that she worried about Calvin, that he was a good fella but that he had a propensity for raising hell, although he never hurt anyone. Then she confessed the horrid details of Big C's killing. She nudged me with her shoulder toward the broken screen door, shoved it open, her upper body extended out of the door, and pointed with her right hand at the spot Big C had died. I felt embarrassed. I heard her confession. Her facial transformation was quick: one minute she was quizzically gazing at a strange white man standing in her living room, engaging in a cash negotiation, and the next she was staring off in a mournful contemplative way.

So intimate, so painful, tendered to me, an outsider, a white man, a stranger. Her voice, so dominant, so domineering minutes ago, now was gravelly. Eyes moistened.

"He was a three-star Vice Lord," she said with pride. "I got others to take care of now. . . . Fat motherfucker, Twon. If them cops left him on the street, I'd a killed him."

Memphis, a Vice Lord, was a veteran of the state's prison system, a prisoner of heroin addiction. He never talked about Big C or his killing. Avoiding mention of the name of the dead is a common proscription in many cultures.

Big C's name had been etched onto Mo's forearm with a sewing needle and liquid blue ink. Once, just once, she allowed me to see it. The dusty spot where Big C lay dead was an unmarked grave, close to the Washingtons' front door, which was always open to welcome him back home.

Death

"If I meet only one young woman on the north end, who should I meet?" I asked Iresha, a few weeks after Burpee introduced me to the Washington family. ReRe chuckled. We walked to Nike's apartment, in early evening, across the erstwhile green space at the center of the Pines. It was cold, fall had ended and winter begun. Iresha knocked.

Nike answered. Iresha introduced me. I shook Nike's hand. I told her I'd like to visit her soon. A dub served as bait. She agreed. Iresha warned me that Nike had a furious temper.

I returned a few weeks later. Nike was fourteen. Her mother stayed in the apartment. Nike told her mother to leave us alone, ordering her into her bedroom. "And close the door." My first question was "Nike, what's your earliest memory?" Nike wasn't taken aback, nor did she hesitate to answer the question. She jumped ahead to answer questions I hadn't yet asked. Nike told me she hated her mother, that one day her mother grabbed the baseball bat that stood leaning against the wall behind the kitchen door, drew it back and swung, hitting Nike in the head, knocking her unconscious onto the kitchen floor. She was twelve years old at the time. Her mother smacked her often.

A few months later, I knocked on her door to visit again. I used a friendly knock. No one answered. I tried a cop knock. No response. Nike's neighbor Ericka heard me knocking. She and her preschool children stayed in the apartment adjacent to Nike's. She stuck her head out of the front door, looked left and saw me standing at Nike's door. "Mark, she ain't home." She went on to say that Nike had been arrested, convicted, and sentenced to prison. Ericka wasn't sure of the charge. She did know that Nike "got caught up in something bad. I don' know when she be home." Two years later I heard a rumor that Nike had returned home to the Pines. By the time we met the second time, her son, Charles, was about a year old.

Nike's mother didn't like me at all. She didn't trust me around the apartment and worried when I was there and she and Nike had to dig into their cash box, a cigar box holding dimes and dubs, earnings harvested by their backdoor weed business. Nike was nonchalant about me hanging around. I would horse around with her son and watch television. It was a good spot to hang out. Nike's friends wandered in, did business, or just watched television and gossiped. When Nike wasn't looking, I'd turn down the sound. Nike blamed her son. She'd turn up the sound, again. I thought Nike might punish Charles. I confessed. "Keep your fucking hands off it." I obeyed.

Nike's mother smoked cigarettes, lighting a fresh one off the short end of one she had just finished. Their apartment fogged up. It was impossible to breathe fresh air. I nagged Nike so much about second-hand cigarette smoke's effect on her son's health that she eventually told her mother to smoke in her bedroom. Her mama hated me even more after that, if that was possible.

Nike's mother became gravely ill, lung disease. Her mama, at least to my eye, didn't look healthy even before lung disease had been diagnosed. Chain-smoking had deeply creased her facial skin, and a yellowish patina had formed on her cigarette-holding fingers. She moved at a snail's speed around the apartment, had a gravelly voice, and a hacking cough. After she was hospitalized, Nike implored me to drive her to the hospital to visit mama every night. Death came soon.

Nike confronted her mother's death alone. Her baby daddy, home from prison only a few months, attended the funeral. Folks at the Pines contributed cash to cover expenses. Nike mourned quietly.

Local folks didn't commiserate over death. No one offered a shoulder to cry on. Sudden infant death syndrome took several babies. Young mothers talked about circumstances of their babies' death. Tears, hugs of consolation, were absent.

I felt Mo's profound pain over Big C's death.[4] I listened quietly when Mo talked about Big C. Sometimes when I hung around neighborhoods long enough, folks said things to me that were more personal than I'd expect. When I walked into Mo's apartment the first time, a strange white man, I offered her cash. Months passed, cash changed hands. Our relationship matured beyond a cash exchange. She felt something in our interaction I hadn't, something that went beyond the cash exchange. From time to time over the years, Mo recounted the story of the day we met at the Pines. Each retelling got longer and funnier. Over time the expectation of cash transfer faded. It was replaced by something ill defined. Maybe it was friendship or a sense of mutual respect. Maybe it was just that I quietly listened to her.

Immaculate Explosion

One day, like any other, I stopped by the Washingtons' apartment. Two things happened. The first thing was a retelling of the story of the day Mo hoisted a kitchen knife and chased Calvin out of the apartment and down the sidewalk. At each retelling, the knife was longer, the chase down the sidewalk got longer, and Calvin's laughter got louder. The second thing on that day was serious. Mo was pissed off at Calvin. She fumed. I thought she'd burst into flames.

"You know what dem dumb motherfuckers done? Now we getting kicked out of here, gotta move agin. I hate movin'."

"What the fuck did you do?" I inquired. Sounding like the fellas works to tear the robes off of a college professor.

Calvin laid out the incident. He told me about the kid with the handgun who was the cousin of a friend's cousin who had come down from Chicago to visit for a few days, sell dubs, hit on the girls.

A few nights ago, the fellas got high. A few drank forties. Soon a gun appeared. It was passed around like a Christmas toy. Fellas laughed, Calvin said, told stories about their expert knowledge of weapons, meanwhile hitting a fat blunt and passing a forty. The way Calvin told the story Slim teased the hell out of Shibazz, claiming he didn't know anything about handguns, all the while chastising him, shouting that he shouldn't have had a pistol, that he was fool, that his stupidity could get all of them arrested.

Shibazz endured Slim's harassment for only a proverbial minute. "'Bazz, he hopped up, tore off running after Slim," all in fun, Calvin asserted, threatening to "whup his ass." No one knows how what happened next happened. The pistol 'Bazz carried just happened to discharge, the bullet missing Slim, grazing Calvin's back and digging a U-shaped gouge into the skin near his left scapula. I saw the wound. Calvin was so lucky. A slightly straighter angle, the bullet would have penetrated his chest. He'd likely be dead. No one remembered the details of the immaculate explosion, the forties and blunts clouded the fellas' collective memory. The pistol, Calvin reiterated, "it just went off."

When Calvin told me about the incident, I knew why Burpee was emphatic in his demand that I call him when I arrived on the north end. I had bought insurance. Even so, Burpee couldn't prevent accidents.

Not long after the immaculate explosion, the Washington family was evicted, shamefully kicked out of the Pines, a place where they had a convenient social life. Neighbors were friends who hung out outside in warm weather and inside in cold weather. Mo busied herself with gossiping and looking after other women's younger kids as they played on the common areas and in her living room, television blasting loud enough to be heard on Green Street. She growled at the kids when they were too noisy. Everyone went home unharmed.

Friends Nearby

The Pines appeared to outsiders, as it did to me at first, to be a run-down, low-rent, public housing project depleted of things people need for a rich social life. Appearances are deceptive. I didn't grasp the depth of the social life at the Pines when I first started hanging out with the Washington family and Nike and Ericka and their friends. A woman walking ninety feet, the distance from the Washingtons' apartment to the six-car parking lot, is likely to talk to three, four, or five friends on the way there and another three, four, or five different friends on the way back. When the kids' playground was erected near the front entrance, it became a magnet, attracting mothers, grammas, aunties, and teenage girls with baby carriages. Boys hung out at a distance, watching the teenage girls.

Once I knew the people by sight or name, I paid attention to who chatted with whom. I recognized the mothers of children playing. Hanging out, chatting, and gossiping were social interactions among women who supported one another. Just simply chatting in the evening while their children played made it clear that folks were not alone. There were young mothers with three or four children who moved out of the cramped quarters in the Pines to roomier Section 8 apartments and houses, several blocks or a quarter mile or more away. Once the thrill of extra space wore off, the recognition of loss settled in. Women's friends weren't in the next room or next building or across the grassy public spaces. Women without cars had no means to visit their now far-away friends. Women with cars and kids in Section 8 housing didn't have the desire to load kids and their stuff into cars, drive even a relatively short distance, only to unload kids and kids' stuff, merely to chat, then reload and drive home to their empty houses.

The Pines was a community of women and children who shared social pleasures of daily life. Women who moved into a Section 8 houses or apartments lost those social interactions, the friendships, the personal contacts, the time spent together talking and watching one another's children. The culture of community life was a solution to personal loneliness and remedied childcare duties with an abundance of grammas, mothers, and aunties always ready to watch kids play. Women needed those interactions to stay socially vigilant, watch out for one another, and feel like they were members of a community of women, an extended family of fictive kin.

5

New Neighbors

Memphis searched out a new place to stay and found it across the tracks on a quiet, tree-lined street. The Washington family settled into the Blue House, a stone's throw west of the Pines. The Fence, a local purveyor of goods whose unknown provenance mattered not to his customers, stayed nearby. On warm days the Fence grilled lunches, offering burgers to anyone who walked up or drove by. He was known locally for his outstanding ribs. Customers dined in his grassy yard, enjoying the sunshine. Smoking was permitted. BYOB. Occasionally local fellas dropped by with a few forties, relaxed on picnic table seating, lit up, and enjoyed an assortment of intoxicants.

I delighted in watching folks drive up and park in a short driveway under a mature tree with expansive branches on the north side of the Fence's house. Folks walked up and knocked on the door. It opened slightly. They stepped inside. Some carried away small bags. Some walked away without bags. They placed an order. Cops occasionally parked in that driveway on the north side of the house, when they wanted to watch the open-air drug market across the street. Cops didn't order lunch.

In early September, I wanted to place an order. I walked up to the anchor fence wrapped around the outdoor seating. "I need to talk you, okay?" He shrugged, walked away. He didn't respond. "Come on, man, you know me. You know me. I'm not a cop. You see me a lot across the street. You're not in jail, are you?"

I asked him how long it would take to get a single-lens reflex (SLR) camera, a birthday present for my daughter whose birthday was a month away. He said some goods like those hanging on shelf hooks and sealed in hard plastic containers in places like Target are easy to pilfer. If I wanted one of those, he'd have it in a few days. An SLR, he said, was harder to get, if it was at all possible. SLRs are kept behind counters in glass cases, he said. He'd give it the old college try. He'd need at least a month's notice. I offered a down payment. I waited weeks, checked in now and then on progress. He couldn't get an SLR. The risk of getting pinched was too high, he said.

I knew he couldn't get an SLR. He told me that the day I asked him for the SLR a month earlier. He'd forgotten. I didn't want a hot SLR nor did I want to get pinched with hot goods. I wanted to learn how the operation worked. If you want to learn about weddings you go to the rehearsal.

Patti's Drug House and Ice Cream Store

Off a few blocks east of the Blue House, Tracy's elder sister Patti operated a drug house and ice cream store. Tracy and Cliff hole up in an empty garage, a few blocks away from Patti's, decked out with a twin bed, a thin wool blanket, whitish sheets, a wooden kitchen table with two legs shorter than the others, and three armless wood chairs in desperate need of paint. Use of a toilet and a tub required a dash to the main house, which was guarded by a quadruped, thankfully chained to a pipe implanted deeply into the front yard. The quadruped barked viciously when anyone—friends, cops, or tweekers—dared to penetrate the chain-link fence encircling the property.

An elderly lady folks called Mama owned Patti's house, an abandoned church adjacent to Patti's, a corner house half a block east of Patti's, and an abandoned church at the end of the block. Patti looked like a run-of-the-mill PTA mom. A few minor drug beefs long ago, nothing major, no big deal. No tats. She would launch into a frenzied lecture on the use of proper English near children and a church if four-letter words were uttered within earshot.

Mama, a spry woman in her seventies in search of her next husband, was not, she said, afraid of Byron and his Vice Lord friends down the block to the east. Mama was a cougar long before cougars were cool. We met on a warm midweek school day in August. Patti and I were standing on her front lawn waiting for her son Ty, a high school senior, to arrive at home after football practice. I saw him walking on the opposite sidewalk, hauling football gear and a backpack. He made sure his shoulder pads stuck out of his gym bag. Ty walked over to us, looking tired. His backpack was loaded with textbooks and homework assignments. Patti introduced me to Ty. We shook hands. Small talk quickly came to an end when Patti told him I was a college teacher.

Ty told me his dream, playing Division 1 college football. I told him ancient stories about my years at Washington State University, where I taught dozens of football players on the Cougars 1981 Holiday Bowl and 1988 Aloha Bowl teams. A few of my student football players graduated college and entered the NFL. He was impressed. Ty asked about university classes, the number of hours devoted to homework, and how players manage football requirements in addition to university academics. Junior, Patti's youngest son, soon came along and joined us. His interest leaned toward the ice cream sold on the porch.

Mama picked up trash in the yard, moving slowly, grabbing a cigarette butt, then another, and paper scraps.[1] She was quite limber, bending at the waist, scooping up debris left behind by discourteous teenagers, she said. She grew louder and angrier, mumbling and grumbling in a conspicuously loud voice, cursing and yelling about the stinky trash and empty soda cans and cigarette butts on the front lawn of the house Patti and her sons rented from her. Mama aimed the rental information at me. She was the boss. She wanted me to know it. Most of all, Mama was so very pissed off that Patti hadn't introduced her to me. I took the blame. I told her it was quite rude of me, to stand in her yard—a yard I didn't know she owned—and fail to introduce myself. With contrition came forgiveness. Mama and I, along with Ty and Junior, picked up soda cans and cigarette butts in the yard, and at Mama's instruction, we moved into the gutter, where we picked up more trash. Mama had a reputation on the block. She growled at folks who didn't pick up trash that was tossed about their yard and bitched at them if their grass grew too long. She complained mightily if homeowners allowed teenagers to hang out in or near their yards at night smoking blunts. She insisted that homeowners chase those teens away, bringing a baseball bat, if necessary, and 911 'em but not shoot anyone.

On the front porch of the house Patti rented from Mama, Patti ran her store. Partitioned off by unbreakable see-through partitions and secured with a padlock the size of cantaloupe, the store offered canned generic soda, many colors and flavors of frozen ice, and a small array of chips. Mama's specialty, she proudly announced, were ices she made at home. On summer days, youngsters one after another hopped up the three wooden front steps, bought ices, soda, and junk food, and ran off, dropping chip bags, soda cans, and ice cream wrappers on the yard, which kept Mama busy and so pissed that she felt she had the right to loudly complain.

Patti's front lawn was a gathering place for kids on bikes, who chased one another around the yard and into the street. Adults hanging out on the steps, smoking cigarettes, quietly chatting, asked me if I'd lend them money to buy soda. The clever moochers waited until I bought a cold soda, then yelled at me to buy them one. While I hung around talking or stood on the porch, buying cans of generic soda or watching the street, men and women walked past me. There was no eye contact. Men and women I hadn't seen before that day or the day before and didn't see afterward walked onto the porch, turned to look at the street, opened the door, and glided inside a darkened living room. There, they stayed for hours, tucked away in the dark recesses imbibing their favorite mind-altering concoctions.

Drugs Kill

Byron and his fellas down the street sold illegal commodities. Their greed caused them grave misfortune.

Folks nearby talked about that killing, although no one on that block claimed to have seen firsthand what happened, nor would they, even if they had watched the incident from living room windows in nearby houses. What follows here is Patti's version of the incident, supplemented by others' thoughts about the stupidity of the townie coming down there to cop.

In the middle of a dark street, fearful of cops pulling up behind you, you slip a dub into an empty palm of a man whose face you don't see. He in turn slips a baggie into your palm. You conceal it in your fist, stash it under your seat, or stick it down your pants into your underwear, slide up your window, and gun it before you're busted. You were warned about that black neighborhood. It took guts to drive up in there just before midnight and cop the goods. You are pleased you were able to drive away, still in one piece, unscathed.

You get back to your house, hide in a room with your mates, grab the whitish marble-sized $20-item you so highly desired, stick it in the end of a glass tube against a wire mesh backstop, and fire away. Nothing happens. It doesn't light. You roll it out of the tube, look at it under a lamp light. "Motherfucker." It's drywall. Pissed off, you tell your mates you're going back down there, going to kick ass until you get what you paid for. No one volunteers to accompany you on your ass-kicking retribution adventure.

You're angry at getting hustled, you pull up at the spot where you were ripped off. Slide down your window. Dude walks up. You complain loudly, demand that either you get your money back or that the drywall be exchanged for the real deal rock cocaine you thought you bought. "Get the fuck out of here, 'fore you get hurt." Words heat up. Adrenaline pumps. You feel that you can handle yourself. Loud voices blended into the night air. Obscenities are shouted. The car door flies open. The indignant customer steps out. Later he's found dead in the middle of street.

Folks on the block are puzzled. Why'd that college boy come up in here? Why'd he get out of his car? Why'd he raise his hands? No one 911'ed. Folks returned to whatever they were doing. The block got quiet again. Hours passed before someone on the block driving down the street spotted the body.

The customer's death didn't slow business at Patti's. Time passed. Patti's block and several others eventually were met with a reaction from law enforcement that hit the neighborhood like a freight train hurtling down the tracks. In an instant, there were sirens, flashing colored lights, handcuffs, weapons, and everything changed. Her drug emporium was busted, the house boarded up, Patti imprisoned. Sentencing guidelines were unkind. Folks on the street said she was doing at least a dime, ten years plus.

A Hurtling Freight Train

On Mother's Day government support checks arrive. On warm summer nights the street gets busy in late afternoon and busier into the evening. Drug spots pop up, folks drive or walk to pick up a dime or a dub or to just hang out and catch up on goings-on. Buyers cruise up, buy a product, and off they go.

Ex-cons show up at drug spots. They're easy to spot, covered with prison ink, wandering up like they just so happened to find a drug spot they didn't know was there, strolling around the same way they walked a prison rec yard on sunny days, head on a swivel, eyes moving side to side, looking around, heading off danger.

Motorcycles rumble up. A crowd gathers. Drug selling takes a back seat to telling jokes to keep folks amused. To an outsider, drug spots look like a social gathering on a warm afternoon. Friends mingle. Men and women back on the streets from prison circulate in the crowd, to be seen, to see if mates of former years are back yet. The scene described next occurred in front of the Blue House, shortly before the Washington family vacated it.

Friday, a warm spring afternoon, a patrol car stopped half a block south of the congregation of sellers and buyers and folks mingling. The cop sat behind the wheel, watching patiently. The congregation was aware that the law was down the street, but it nevertheless seemed unfazed. Half an hour passed. The cop cruised by. He looked at sellers and buyers and bystanders. They looked back. He drove off. Later in the evening, the cop returned. This time he parked his car nose out in a driveway across the street from the congregation. There he sat, watching. Time passed. The congregation was smaller than it had been six hours earlier. Folks stood together being watched. Later, just before mid-night, the congregation disassembled. Cop disappeared.

The cop and the congregation met that way each Friday afternoon for about a month. Nothing changed. The drug store stayed opened. Then, after a few weeks of obvious warnings, at five in the morning on a Saturday, the law enforcement freight train hurtled in. Helicopters dropped in. Patrol cars swooped in. Sellers, parole violators, folks wanted on warrants were carted off in handcuffs. Only a few returned days later. Others, folks said, would return in five to ten years with good behavior.

City workers erected a children's playground on the west end of that block. It was a thoughtful addition to the area. It attracted youngsters and their mothers. Nearby a sign was erected announcing that selling drugs within some number of feet near the park would bring the world crashing down on the drug sellers.

Warning to Wrongdoers

Drug policing was an incredible event to watch. The police made the future predictable. I couldn't believe my eyes. The police couldn't have made it clearer if they held up a sign: "You are selling illegal drugs. Cops are watching. You will be arrested, convicted, and imprisoned. Go home, now!"

Look! There's a patrol car. An officer sits behind the wheel, watching. There are a few drug sellers pitching their wares, walking from the curb into the street, handing drugs to buyers copping. Other folks are congre-gated, hanging out chattering and laughing—not all people hanging out at a drug spot sell drugs.

The scene reminded me of a natural history documentary. We see an antelope grazing at a water hole. Lions are lying in the grass, nearby, watching. Now and then a few lions stroll by the antelope grazing and lapping up water. Antelope are blasé, they see the lions stroll by but cannot foresee the looming attack.

There they were on the street between the Fence and the Blue House, the hunters and the hunted, looking at each other. The hunted didn't move. The hunter watched. I thought to myself, "Don't you know who's watching? Do what you have to do, just don't be stupid. Look, cops are watching."

The Washington boys hung around when the patrol car first rolled by. I shooed them away, told them to go inside and do homework. They objected. I won out. They, like everyone there, enjoyed hanging out. I did too. So did the neighborhood folks, teenaged and young adult men and women, and ex-cons. Drug selling was a single act in a larger social occasion on that warm sunny day. Most people weren't pushing anything but tall tales.

The hunter sent a message loud and clear in a manner consistent with the spirit of a university town. Tell people what you want them to do. Give them a few chances to do it. Then, if they don't do it, give them an F. In this instance, there was one grade: A, as in "arrested."

Champaign didn't approve of police personnel attacking law breakers with ferocious dogs, busting down doors with armed gizmos, or sending in storm troopers wearing knee-high black leather boots, helmets, and face masks. If that type of policing happened, I didn't see or hear about it.

Champaign's community culture promotes harm-reduction policing. The community and its police department recognize people use and sell illegal drugs, as it recognizes that underage college students drink alcohol and smoke weed. Police can't throw all of them in jail. The police can and do send an unambiguous message. *We're here. We're coming. Stop selling drugs. Stop doing whatever you're doing that's illegal. We know about it. Just stop! Or do it in a place we cannot see you doing it.*

Hustlers like those who were busted when the law enforcement freight train hurtled through the north end, cuffing and taking offenders away, are addicts. They're addicted to action. Rumor held that most of those who went to jail had been there before. Many were on parole. Even if lawbreakers get careless, the street's hard, prison's easy.

The north end community didn't feel mistreated that day by law enforcement. North end chatter didn't hash and rehash the bust or distort police tactics or cast blame on the police for arresting innocents. Local culture accepts economic and social reality. The north end community knows folks sell illegal drugs to keep their heads above financial water. If folks need to sell drugs to buy food and diapers, it's ok, but don't do it within public view. Keep it quiet. This community absorbs convicted felons into its daily social order. It leaves room for them, too, to do as they wish, within limits.

Burpee saw the drug bust this way. Illegal drug sellers know they will get busted, arrested, convicted, and imprisoned—that goes along with a drug hustle. Drug dealers know it; they have no right to complain when they get busted.

Harm-reduction policing fits well within Champaign community culture and within the culture of the north end, a culture shaped by anti-black violence, racial discrimination, and the economic fate of being locked out of decent employment. Burpee's life history captures the essence of the difficult lives of north end's older men and women: born in abject poverty in Chicago and reared in an urban environment surrounded by whites who hate blacks. The north end community shares a history of memories of horrible lives, deliberate discrimination, and racial victimization. North end culture that I saw adjusted to that abhorrent history. Local culture adopted harm-reduction values similar to the policing strategy. Do whatever you wish, but don't harm others in violent ways. Recognize that offensive behavior endangers others. Accept the consequences.

The Blue House

Housing authority rules prohibited pets. Now that the family was no longer in publicly subsidized housing, Calvin decided he needed a pet. Calvin chose a nasty, growling wolflike canine that, to me, appeared to be an instance of a genetic regression to a period in canine evolution when dogs were thoroughly undomesticated, uncivilized, and downright dangerous. Calvin's pet was a subspecies of canine like the quadruped in the front yard of the place where Tracy and Cliff had stayed. He locked up that beast behind the house, in a six-foot high anchor-fence enclosure. That fence needed bails of razor wire hung along the top. I still didn't feel safe. Nice pet.

I would walk up the short sidewalk to the front porch, and that nasty creature would bark and snarl and jump up onto the enclosure, exposing its man-eating canines. I prayed that the fence would hold steady. I despised that creature. Calvin hooked up the creature's collar to a chain that, in my opinion, could never have too many sufficiently massive links. No one else seemed to mind its growling, barking, and pooping all over the sidewalk and lawn.

Life at the Blue House lasted half a year or thereabouts. Memphis told me there were plumbing problems. It wasn't funny, though I couldn't help myself from laughing, that the upstairs toilet rocked side to side and tilted back and forth like a carnival ride when someone sat on it.

Memphis the Unshakable was nonplussed by goings on around him. A tilting, rocking, swaying toilet didn't bother him as long as it kept flushing. It flushed okay, although it leaked. Water had seeped along the hose connecting the toilet tank to the water supply. Water slid down the wall behind the tank onto the floor. That slow cascade had likely been happening over years. Water infiltrated decades-old and by now rotted plywood flooring.

Memphis the Persistent repeatedly called his absentee landlord, who never answered the phone. Memphis spoke to the answering machine, recorded goings-on with the tilting toilet, the stream of water seeping day and night, the rotted floor. Eventually, the landlord returned his calls. The landlord told Memphis a repair crew would soon remedy the tilting toilet and repair the rotted floor. The repair crew was as hard to track down as the absentee landlord.

Memphis the Tolerant waited, waited, waited. He called again and again. No response. No repairmen. The toilet kept tilting. Water dripped through the rotted floor, onto the floor joists and down onto the plaster ceiling below, seeping through it and onto the first floor.

Bless his heart, Memphis the Believer waited, waited, and waited. Memphis said he had slowly acquired a religious sense of the goodness of people. He believed the landlord would do the right thing.

I reached out, telling Burpee about the tilting toilet, the rotted floor, the water dripping onto the first floor. Burpee, the ever-impatient man, offered the kind of help that a landlord like Memphis's demanded. He volunteered to send his boys to talk to the landlord. He guaranteed that after that conversation, the toilet would get fixed. Burpee asked me to ask Memphis where to find the landlord.

"Where's the landlord? You said he lived out of town. Do you know where?" Memphis shrugged. He didn't know. He had faith the guy would send a repair crew.

On a quiet evening Bennie and Willie were engaged in homework. Calvin was out back taming the savage beast. Mo had wandered off somewhere in the neighborhood. A mini-mission. Memphis was shuffling around the kitchen, cooking dinner. He heard a loud, dull THUD. He said it sounded like a heavy object had smashed into the first floor. And indeed, that's what had happened. The second-floor toilet now rested without a tilt on the first floor. Water trickled through the gaping hole in the ceiling. Memphis turned off the water leading to the hose that led to the toilet tank that now sat on the first floor. Luckily, the toilet's water supply had shut-off valves.

Memphis called the landlord. He reported that the second-floor toilet had crashed through the floor and that it now rested on the first floor. How lucky it was that no one was killed. His landlord did not respond.

Memphis set out on a house search, a task he knew well. He needed housing quickly. Fall was turning into winter. The Blue House wasn't properly outfitted. Cold wind blew through closed windows. I mentioned to Memphis that the roof might not be strong enough to handle three or four feet of snow piled atop rotting shingles and rotted underlayment.

The Women's Shelter

When the toilet dropped into the living room like a meteor hurtling through the floor, Memphis needed to find new accommodations.

He searched the town in his battered, powder blue pickup truck. He let me join him. I thought his pickup was a wonderful example of the durability of American engineering. Rusty doors didn't close fully. It had one windshield wiper. Oil fumes shot out of the exhaust pipe. The stick shift on the floor had to be double-clutched to shift gears. The bench-style front seat's fibrous filling, probably asbestos, pushed out of cracks and holes in the vinyl. Old metal cranks didn't fully close the windows. A radio of the President Kennedy era had stopped playing way back in the day. Memphis adored his truck. He even washed it! I coveted his truck.

Across town, Preacher Harris, a friend of Burpee's, had been successfully operating a full-service faith-based women's shelter over many years. Preacher used his influence and amassed sufficient resources to rehabilitate an abandoned 1960-ish motel that would serve as a respite, a safe housing project to protect alcoholic and drug-addicted women on the mend and their children from drug sellers and abusive boyfriends. The shelter was supported by donations from community organizations, private citizens, and grants, illustrating the community's willingness to help those in need. In its heyday, the motel seemed to have been a decent place to spend a night while driving through town. I had memories of cheap-end motels like this one in travels with my parents when I was a boy. The reception area had been transformed into offices, a dining room, and a chapel. Women residents rehabbed rooms, one by one. They stripped wallpaper, replaced it with new paint, scrubbed bathtubs and toilets, washed down walls, vacuumed carpets, and pulled out years of filth and grim. Broken plumbing fixtures were replaced, rot was repaired. No tilting, rocking toilets there.

Rooms were arranged into four, two-story rows set in a north-south direction. The western-most row had a family room on the second floor. Upper floor rooms were safer, with fewer break-ins. The wall separating two single rooms had been knocked out, leaving space adequate to sleep at least four people. There were two bathrooms. One of the two original entry doors was replaced by a wall.

Protecting women and children's privacy and keeping them secure posed a serious challenge if the property's perimeter wasn't secured at night. Drug sellers had been creeping onto the property in the wee hours, enticing women to buy illegal drugs or offering them a drugs-for-sex exchange. Preacher needed a solution. Security systems and extra lighting were well outside the financial reach of the shelter.

Burpee solved the preacher's security problem. Alabama had come to town after twenty years locked up in nasty hellhole prisons like Stateville. Burpee gave Alabama his first out-of-prison employment opportunity. He replaced Alabama's prison garb with civvies. He kept his prison boots, which were thick soled and ankle high, perfect for kicking unwanted men off the property.

"Mark, this is Alabama."

I greeted him and extended my hand. Handshakes are atypical in prisons. Convicts don't shake hands with one another. Prison staff and convicts most definitely don't shake hands. I knew that. That's why I reached out to Alabama to shake his hand. It's off-putting. It's a necessary mannerism to learn after twenty years in prison. Alabama smiled, lowered his eyes, averting his from mine. A bit reluctant to shake my hand, a bit shy, he reached out anyway. His right hand had the dimensions of a doormat. That massive hunk of flesh with fingers enclosed my hand. His light squeeze felt like the tightening grip of a blood-pressure cuff.

Exiting prison after twenty years was traumatizing. Burpee found Alabama a spot, an apartment near his house. He needed to stay close, to keep an eye on Alabama. After Alabama was settled in his abode, Burpee introduced the preacher to him. Preacher's forehead reached Alabama's sternum. His first post-prison full-time job was his first-ever straight job. Alabama's skillset was a perfect match to the job description: keep drug sellers and suspicious vehicles off the parking lot between dusk and dawn.

Alabama performed well. It wasn't long, maybe only a few days actually, before drug sellers got the message. They stopped trying to creep the property under a shroud of darkness. A few "tried" Alabama. Those fools found themselves looking up at a man the size of Bigfoot. Rumor held that a few creepers tried to bully and threaten Alabama. Those hustlers ended up battered, bruised, and searching out new venues.

Near the end of the Washington family's stay at the women's shelter, a white boy about sixteen showed up. He'd absconded on probation in Kentucky. He fled north to hang out, to hide at his auntie's house. First time I laid eyes on him was at the women's shelter in late summer. I loathed the little weasel. He had eyes for Iresha. He had eyes of a predator. He had the look of a boy whose charms can woo an inexperienced, sixteen-year-old young lady like Iresha who hadn't yet been exposed to weasels who knock up girls and then when they hear the words "I'm pregnant" flee out of town, out of sight, ignore responsibility, hide from it, as if the sheriff were hunting them.

Time at the women's shelter ended. It was early fall. The weather turned chilly. Green leaves faded into a kaleidoscope of splendid color. Memphis located a house, the White House. Life would be good, again.

The White House

Life was good. Mo was overjoyed. Memphis packed their belongings, loaded them into his baby blue pickup.

The White House was huge; it had lots of bedrooms and bathrooms, no rocking toilets, and massive trees that cast shade over the front and back yard. Best of all, the White House was near the Pines. Mo had friends nearby within easy walking range that made evening missions easy. One thing troubled her.

Mo was beside herself, howling about the neighbors down the block: "Hoes down the block." She grilled poor Memphis, demanding to know why he had rented a house only a few houses away from a whorehouse at the end of the block.

Iresha and Calvin thought living near a whorehouse could be great fun. I thought so too. Nights at that end of the street were busy. The kids took up a watch post on the wraparound front porch. Cars pulled up, men jumped out, ran inside, ran out in less than ten minutes, sped off, hoping to evade police, if any happened to be busting houses of prostitution.

"Yo, Mark, you see them hoes down the street?"

"Hoes? What hoes, ReRe?"

"Down the end of the block. Down that way," she pointed with her right index finger.

"Really, working girls, down the street. That's funny."

"Why don't you walk down there. See what they look like. They white girls."

"You haven't seen them?"

She rolled her eyes, crunched up her face. "Me, why would I go see them? Dem ugly white bitches."

"Hey, folks got to make a living."

"That's just wrong, Mark. Sell weed's okay, but ho'ing? That's just wrong."

The White House was a step up in accommodations after living in one room in the women's shelter and before that dealing with an unresponsive absentee landlord and an airborne toilet. Calvin fancied another ferocious quadruped. That desire Mo quickly kiboshed. "Huhuh, we don't have money to feed no dog. You get a job. You buy the food." The thought of getting a job was a sufficient deterrent. Spending hard-earned money on dog food, Calvin thought, was a waste of cash better used to invest in weed.

The wooden wraparound porch had a width sufficient to welcome at least three-dozen visitors. Front columns gave the place a sense of old-time stately grandeur. The front door had a window about two-feet square covered with a strip of a bed sheet stapled to the door frame. A wide staircase covered by a threadbare carpet led from the entry to three upper floors. To the right of the entryway was the living room, which appeared to be at least twenty by twelve feet. A small-screen television atop a wooden box had a place on a shaky wooden table. A four-cushion beige couch separated the entry and living room. It was positioned to allow television viewing.

On the front side of the living room there was a semicircular alcove. Someone in town told me alcoves like that one in the Washingtons' house were designed for viewing the dead, which I thought was rather creepy. The alcove was large enough to hold a coffin. The porch was sufficiently lengthy to allow dozens of well-wishers to pass by and view the deceased lying in the living room in the coffin. I did not share with the family that particular theory of the living room alcove.

The kitchen matched the length of the living room, about twenty feet long, and held old, still-operable equipment. The ancient refrigerator had a thick, heavy door. Inside, there was enough storage space to hold food supplies sufficient to feed a hundred-yard-long line of visitors waiting to view the deceased in the coffin alcove.

A freezer chest was pushed against the living room side of the wall that separated the living room and kitchen. Memphis was about six feet tall. When he opened the freezer lid to grab frozen meat and fish, he needed the full length of his upper body and long arms to make the grab. The freezer box scared me. It had a lock contraption the size of a five-pound pumpkin. That type of freezer was outlawed decades ago. Children playing in and around these freezers got themselves trapped inside, suffocated. I'd seen similar freezers in movies about killers who stored their victims in a freezer. Memphis's freezer might easily conceal three thin or two beer-bellied dead guys.

During daylight hours the family members weren't at home. Boys had school. Iresha wandered about the streets. LaWanda visited Mario, a parolee purported to be her husband. He stayed in his gramma's house, east and south of the Pines. It was outside the central area of the north end, not too far from the road that separated Champaign and Urbana.

Big C was dead. I knew Calvin, Bennie, and Willie. I had met Mario the Lazy. The only male family member I hadn't met was Jason. No one mentioned him until the family moved from the women's shelter to the White House. Mo and Iresha warned me about Jason. Mo told me to stay away, don't come into the house if he's there. Iresha nodded her agreement. In a few weeks, that violent and unpredictable man would be paroled. "He's a racist. He don' like whites. Stay away when he comes home." I didn't heed Mo's warning. I met Jason on a midweek evening.

Bennie answered the door, laughing, teasing me yet again about knocking like a cop. Mo was standing in the living room. She shot me a look like she'd seen an evil spirit, a clear warning to watch out for Jason. He was sitting on the left-center cushion of the four-cushion couch. Iresha, Bennie, and Willie squeezed together to his left. I stood at the end of the couch on the coffin side of the living room.

Memphis ignored the whole affair, pretending as if Jason the White Hater wasn't sitting in a room where I was standing. He went about his business, walked out of the kitchen to grab frozen food in the freezer in the living room. He leaned into the freezer, the dangerous one, suitable for cadaver storage. Chuckling about how many fat or thin or beer-bellied or chubby guys might fit in the freezer became on ongoing source of humor Memphis and I shared. Memphis pulled himself out of the freezer, held up a gallon-sized bag of frozen shrimp. He walked into the kitchen, looked at me, and said, "Wanna eat dinner?" Thanking him politely, I declined. "Thanks, I ate already." He was a clever man. His offer to feed me sent Jason a message as long as Jason was wise enough to pick up on the message.

I sidled in front of Jason, still seated on the couch among his siblings. I greeted him. "I'm Mark. Your mom said you'd be coming home soon. Must feel good, huh?" He offered a meager "yeah." I reached out to shake his hand. His was cold and stiffly pliable, rather cadaverous, actually.

He stared at me like I was a creature newly descended from a strange planet. "You have a nice family." I offered a kind word. He sat quietly, said nothing, numb, corpselike. The anxiety in the kids' eyes faded, presumably because he didn't attack me.

"Sure you don't want to eat?" Memphis the Vigilant saved me at just the right moment and gave me a reason to move away from Jason and join Memphis in the kitchen.

Memphis, a good-hearted guy, had no idea how to cook. I watched him drop frozen globs of some ilk of seafood with bits and pieces of ice chunks still stuck to the breading into hot oil. Splatters of hot oil shot out of the pan like fireworks. When I saw him holding yet another handful of icy globs over a pressure cooker of boiling oil, I retreated, backed away, and resorted to small-talking about fish recipes and whether he thought the takeout fish joint across the street from the funeral home down the street from the Pines was a good spot.

I was killing time, knowing that Jason wouldn't hang around too much longer with a white man hovering in the kitchen. He didn't. I admit it. I enjoyed irritating him.

He didn't hang around the neighborhood too long, either. I saw him again from time to time at the park a few blocks south of the Pines. I'd wave, yell "Hey." He mellowed with time outside the stress of cellblocks.

He hooked up, got himself a girlfriend with children, a common first move after an ex-convict gets back on the street. He moved into her apartment, ate her food, smoked her weed, and spent her money, refused to get a job. Six months later her continued complaints about him "laying up" all day and doing nothing while she worked got the best of him. He was busted on a domestic violence beef, a bad move if his goal had been to stay on the street. He went back again to state prison to finish his sentence, a huge relief of the Washington family. Jason won't be coming home any time soon.

Bennie and Willie relaxed. They were so pleased. When Jason was hauled off to prison, Bennie and Willie regained the twin bed they had lost when Jason came home. Now that he went back to prison, they had their bed, again. They snuggled together under thin blankets, keeping warm in a barn-sized house with only a moderate heating capacity.

6

Dreams
and Realities

The Washington family space at the women's shelter was cozy. The rectangular double room had an east-facing exterior wall that held the outside door. On the west wall there were two bathrooms. Two queen-sized beds butted against the south wall. The north wall had windows that exposed a view of nearby agricultural fields and in the distance the interstate highway.

Memphis and Mo, three sons, and two daughters managed well in tight spaces. They enjoyed the physical and social closeness. Two round tables were stuck in corners: one served as a desk where the boys piled their school books and did homework, the other held a television and a chess board and a Scrabble game. Bennie, an honor student, taught himself chess. He and his dad enjoyed the competition. Memphis learned to play in prison dayrooms.

I enjoyed casual time with the family. I'd come by this spot like I did at the Pines, in the evening to say hi, hang out, listen to Mo tell stories, tease Bennie about getting his first girlfriend, chat with Iresha about hooping on the Wolverines women's basketball team.

Bennie and Willie were doing well at school. They won achievement awards and proudly displayed these when I walked into the house. They studied. They succeeded.

Bennie, a nice young man, with bright eyes, was verbally adept and asked a lot of questions about college, how hard it was, how much work he'd have to do. He also usually asked, "You think I can do it?" "Keep studying, Bennie, you'll be smarter than the rest," I replied. I meant it.

LaWanda had no future plans, no dreams beyond the confines of the north end. She dreamed of a stable home life like hers growing up. She dropped out of an alternative school after she met Mario. LaWanda talked about Mario and getting married. I could feel Memphis cringe. He didn't openly react to LaWanda's plan to marry Mario. Either he didn't hear or want to acknowledge his daughter's dead-end future with Mario, the lazy ex-convict.

Mo and Memphis wanted their children to finish school, attend college, if that's what the children wanted. Their lives had been tough. Memphis knew that digging the family's way out of the north end would be harder than digging an escape tunnel out of prison. He knew that few escape the lives the north end offers.

Listening to Iresha's and Bennie's dreams, I felt guardedly optimistic that one day they'd escape, find a life outside the north end, returning only to visit their family and friends on annual holidays, that they'd have a life elsewhere, a life that fulfilled them as much as their dreams gave them hope. I was hopeful that the strings that kept kids like Bennie and Iresha held tight to local culture would weaken enough and allow them to escape, pull away, fashion a future outside the community their ancestors settled a century ago. As it turned out, these were my dreams in their behalf, not theirs.

Reality creeps in. Cliff, the ex-con I met near Patti's, nailed it succinctly: "Folks just seem to get caught up." When I looked around the neighborhood, after so many years, I saw that few escaped. People born and raised on north end stayed there. People went to prison from there and returned there. Then again, perhaps it's not that surprising that people stay and that people return: the north end community offers life-long companionship, lots of friends and family, a modest material quality of life, and it's safe. Financial risks were minimal, social attachments strong.

I remembered well one of my first visits to the Pines and the Washington family. We were getting to know each another. I'd stop by to do no more than say hi. Mo or Memphis would invite me inside, or if they weren't there, Calvin or Bennie or Willie would greet me with a smile. "Hey," they'd say. "Come on in. You looking for mom?" That night Calvin let me inside. Memphis and a few middle-aged friends were playing cards on the kitchen table, the type of table you see in old-school diner booths, tables covered by gray Formica with a squiggle design that looks like a chubby version of the Nike swoosh. Memphis sat with his back in the kitchen doorway. He leaned back to see who had come in. He saw me. I walked toward him and leaned on the kitchen wall. I was silent. I didn't want Memphis to think I showed up to badger folks with a barrage of questions. Questions were business. Visiting was personal. I enjoyed the family's company, the energy and warmth of their home.

Memphis looked at his cards and turned his head up toward me and chatted about his children. He made a point of telling me that Iresha would, he was certain, play basketball in college. At nearly six feet, she took after her dad in height. She, like Memphis, shared a casual speaking manner, an easy friendliness, until somebody annoyed her. She was intolerant of fools. When someone got her riled up, she walked away. She had limits, though. She drew a line in the sand, a line well known to the street, a line no one wanted to cross. A tall strong girl with a quick temper: be careful.

When the family was staying at the Blue House, Iresha had been expelled. Fueled by anger, she picked up a chair-desk combination and tossed it through a second-floor window of the alternative school. She told me her teacher had pissed her off. She pleaded her case. By her way of thinking she had used good judgment by throwing the desk instead of the teacher out the window.

Mo and Memphis clearly wanted their children to achieve, although neither of them had, I thought, a sense of what form that academic achievement might take in the long run. Memphis hoped Iresha would secure a place on the University of Michigan's women's basketball team, and both parents were proud of her and her brother Bennie's scores on the Illinois standardized tests. Growing up on the north end makes it hard to know what success looks like outside the neighborhood. Iresha had good test scores, which made me wonder why school authorities focused on her misbehavior and looked past her nascent academic ability.

That night at the Pines over his card game, Memphis and I talked about college. He asked lots of questions about what it's like, how kids gain entrance, and suggested that when the time came, I could help with college applications and put in a good word at my university. A pause came in the conversation, Memphis drifted a bit, and then came back into the reality of the room from wherever he had drifted. "If Iresha gets to her sixteenth birthday without having a baby, I'll be a successful father."

I don't know if Mo and Memphis called their live-in arrangement blissful. It worked. It was a home without violence, except when Mo got pissed off and chased Calvin around, wielding a kitchen knife. She enjoyed the chase more than he enjoyed staying a few feet ahead the blade slashing at his back. A knife scar next to bullet scar, he said, would ruin the look of perfectly good-looking back.

Food was on the table every night. Brothers and sisters and father and mother sat at dinner together, except when Mo went off on a mission. Parents were there, in the house, every day, with their kids. When kids got home from school Memphis or Mo was inside or nearby. The Washingtons' children had a stable family, a life at home.

The Weasel

When the family moved from the women's shelter to the White House, Iresha was still hanging out with the weasel. Many months passed, I knew trouble when I saw it. Mo said there were nights she didn't come home. She was upset. Memphis took it in stride. I knew trouble awaited the family.

Halloween arrived. Costumed kids and their parents were strolling along the sidewalks, tricking or treating on the street near the White House. When I arrived, Mo suggested that I trick or treat at the whore-house. Chuckling, she said, "See what you get."

Over the months Iresha spent with the weasel, I watched her energy drain. She was sluggish; her laughter that was so joyful gradually disappeared; her desire to hang out with friends waned; her desire to be social faded. Her withdrawal wasn't caused by drug use. She never peddled drugs. I never saw her smoke weed or a cigarette. She saw herself as an athlete and needed to respect her body.

By early fall, the weasel stopped coming around to see Iresha. He faded out of sight. Rumor had it that he went back to Kentucky to "handle his business," Memphis said, facing up to absconding on probation and dealing with a warrant for his arrest. Iresha slumped; she was down in the dumps. The weasel had dumped her. After a few weeks, those feelings would pass, I thought. Instead, she grew paler, more listless and lethargic.

Halloween night. The White House. She asked me to drive her to a party. It was an optimistic sign, I thought, that she wanted to spend an evening of laughing and giggling with her friends. We arrived at her friend's home; the girls were standing outside in full party mode. She felt bad. She was nauseous, headachy. I knew what sick teenagers looked like; I had two at home. I offered to take her to an ER visit. She refused, said she'd be okay.

Two days after Halloween I went by the White House to check on her. No one was there. Odd, someone was always there, either in the house or nearby. Memphis's truck was gone. Later that evening still no one was there. Kids on the street hadn't seen Iresha.

Iresha miscarried on Halloween night. She started to bleed at the party. Bleeding worsened as the evening wore on. She called Memphis. He took her to the ER. At home afterward, she still looked exhausted, deeply saddened. A few days passed; her health hadn't recovered. She seemed worse day by day. She developed a fever. She bled, again. Days passed, she worsened. Memphis took her back to the ER. Her womb issued a lifeless fetus.

A Tough Life, a Tough Reality

Iresha and her family recovered. There were no signs of visible commiseration. Mo and Memphis said nothing. They had been about to be grandparents. They hadn't known it. Months passed. The young woman I had known so long shriveled. Her laughter, her bright eyes, her brilliant smile were lost. She stopped hooping at the playground. The trauma she'd experienced caused emotional wounds. Time would heal her, though.

Over the years as I watched Iresha and her younger brothers mature, I slid into the role of a protector, as much as an outsider could. I felt irritated, annoyed, and angry. I had cautioned Memphis and Mo about the weasel, the irresponsible absconder, presaging his pull of Iresha down a dark path. They listened. But Mo said there was little she could do. In their culture, Iresha was "grown," a woman at age sixteen. She had choices. She had made her own decisions. She wouldn't have listened to her parents even if they told her to stay away. She had to live with the consequences of her decisions, like Mo and Memphis had to do when they were her age.

There it was in simple, plain English: Mo's interpretation of their culture's worldview. Teenagers are grown up by their mid-teenage years. Parents gradually let go by age eleven. Teens are on their own. They care for themselves. They attend school or not. They run the streets or not. They smoke or not. They make their own decisions. They live with the consequences. Babies, jail, and prison await those who make poor decisions, at least in my way of thinking.

Those years make teenagers "hard," Burpee told me. Parents prepare children for the reality of the world when it creeps in. Parents aren't abusive, cruel. They aren't neglectful. The streets are tough. Parents allow their children to learn to handle tough times without whining and whimpering. Kids make decisions and are expected to live with the consequences. No excuses. No what-ifs. No it-could-have-been-different-if-only excuses. Teenagers encounter north end culture's reality. Parents' wishes for their children's future remain in the hands of their children. "Folks just get caught up."

Mario and LaWanda

LaWanda and her boyfriend cum fictive husband were hanging out at the Washingtons' apartment at the Pines the first time Burpee escorted me there. Mario was leaning over the handrail on the stairs, peering down to check out the strangers. Soon afterward, he was busted on drug charges, did his time, and was released when the family was living at the women's shelter. LaWanda and Mario were planning to be legally married when his parole ended and he got a job. Mo smirked. Good luck with that. LaWanda visited Mario at his grandmother's spot, where he stayed while on parole. She'd leave Mario Jr. at home with Memphis or Mo, and Memphis or I would drive LaWanda to Mario's.

LaWanda and Iresha and their girlfriends congregated at Mario's gramma's in the afternoon, two or three times a month. Mario's grandmother didn't know the girls hung out there. Weed smoking was not permitted in the house. Stinking up the place with weed smoke was not a good idea; if by an odd quirk of fate his parole officer happened by, it would be serious trouble for Mario.

Sitting around with those girls in the afternoon was a kick. They chattered and laughed, teased one another, and poked fun at the "white man," asking repeatedly why I wasted my time hanging around with them. "Don' you have a job?" There were usually half a dozen girls hanging out, and all of them knew why I hung out. Many had been paid on one or another of my research projects and had helped me find people I wanted to interview or I had interviewed and needed to interview again.

The Washington sisters told me that Mario had doubts about my motives, that he couldn't understand why a college professor would hang around with them and their friends rather than hang out with guys like him and his thug friends. ReRe said Mario thought I was hustling the girls, trying to hook a few of them to work for me as their pimp. That's how little he knew about these young women. I'd heard about a few teenage strippers across town—friends of friends of friends—who had young children and chose to dance as strippers instead of working long hours over longer days to earn what they earned on stage in a few nights. The Washington girls and their friends said they preferred babysitting.

Mario's gramma made his life easy. He had no shopping, cleaning, or cooking duties, and even the idea of job hunting was anathema to him. Mario's only responsibility, he thought, was to tell Brian, his parole officer, that he was looking for work and trying his best to stay clean.

Mario's days were carefree. Midafternoon a few times a week, I'd stop by, bang on his gramma's door just to see who was sitting around inside. I didn't like Mario. He didn't like me. I didn't blame him. If I'd been on parole, I wouldn't have wanted a guy like me hanging around, either. I had prying eyes. Mario was a parasitic parolee, eating his gramma's food, living in her home, promising to find a job he never looked for, while spinning tales LaWanda believed were promises about getting a job and settling down with her and his son. He even bummed weed off his ex-con mates down the street.

I'd seen guys like Mario in one guise or another on the streets in Seattle, Kansas City, and Cleveland and in prison cellblocks. Quite frankly, I was worn out seeing guys like him. It annoyed me that he wouldn't help LaWanda care for Mario Jr. It annoyed me that Mario spent his time watching television, listening to music, eating his gramma's groceries, and sleeping, while his gramma worked ten-hour days in food service on campus. LaWanda was a pleasant and kind albeit naïve young woman. Why she chose a parasite like Mario puzzled me. No matter, she lived with the consequences. "Folks just get caught up." Unfortunately, Mario Jr. did too.

Afternoons on weekdays while gramma worked, he met his fellas and they had a weed smoke-athon in a big ole 1960s variety omnibus Buick parked in the backyard. They ended the smoke-athon in ample time to clean up before his gramma came home around 5 pm, by which time the fellas would have headed back to wherever they were staying. Dressed in a white uniform stained in the colors of food service, she walked into the house around 5:15, looking exhausted, drained. I knew that drained look. My mother worked as a diner waitress when I was a boy. Mario, the slug, didn't even vacuum, wash the kitchen dishes, dust the living room, or kiss his gramma hello when she dragged herself up the four concrete steps and opened the front door of her home.

There's an ironic upside to the LaWanda-Mario story. LaWanda knew her baby daddy. That's not always the case. Mario was a lazy slug, but at least he stuck around. That's rarely the case.

"Who da Baby Daddy?"

Late one afternoon on a warm spring day, I drove five late teenage women to Urbana. Four squeezed onto the back seat of my Passat. Iresha, a lucky girl, rode shotgun. They wanted to visit their nineteen-year-old friend Juicy, a former north end resident, who was pregnant with her second child. On the ride across town, talk of pregnancy and babies filled the air. They giggled about most things and found humor in dark places. That day, the conversation had a serious tone. Someone inquired, "Who Juicy baby daddy?"[1] Simply asking Juicy the name of the baby daddy, I thought, could either be a rude or imprudent question, an embarrassing affront to the about-to-be-new mother, an acceptable cultural option (ask or don't ask), or culturally unnecessary, like asking me, a Jewish man, if I want ham on my cheese sandwich. The conversation went something like this:

"Who Juicy baby daddy?"

"I don't know, was it James?"

"Juicy, how far long?"

"I don't know."

"Four months, I guess."

"Could baby daddy be Jamil?"

"Nah, that means Juicy got pregnant five months ago. Jamil was in jail then."

"Was it Clucker?"

"He just got out of prison after a few years."

"Who'd Juicy have sex with back then four months ago?"

"I remember, she with Darryl, then Maurice."

"No, them guys went away before four months ago."

"It must'a been Rashad. She liked him. He never been to jail."

Juicy's baby daddy didn't hang around during pregnancy nor visit the hospital after his child's birth.[2] The baby daddy, or any man willing to publicly declare biological paternity, didn't sign the birth certificate. Sitting around in Juicy's living room, one of the girls asked if she wanted a third child. She thought for a moment and replied, "Maybe."[3]

Down the street from Patti's in the direction of the tracks, seven late teenage boys and several fellas a few years older who called themselves Vice Lords spent a lot of time hanging out on the concrete stoop and on the sidewalk in front of their rented brick house, which had three small bedrooms, and a ten-by-twelve living room covered with a threadbare, utterly filthy carpet encrusted with dark discolorations. The front door's paint had faded long ago and peeled spots exposed dry rot. Weeds, dirt, rocks, and cigarette butts formed a collage that replaced grass on the front yard. Those fellas were lucky Mama hadn't seen that yard.

On a warm spring day, a few of the fellas who were hanging out on what was supposed to be a grassy strip between the sidewalk and road chatted about girls, sex, and babies. Byron, a chubby fella wearing a whitish T-shirt ripped at the neck, torn at the belly, and in dire need of a thorough scrubbing in a washing machine, carped about his current bitch—his term for his girlfriend—Sylvia. Byron's mate Donnie goaded him, saying he was the baby daddy and, in an ironic way, he casually inquired whether Byron intended to assume paternal responsibilities for his child.

"You going help raise the kid?" Donnie quizzed Byron.

"Hell'nah," exclaimed Byron. His facial expression sent a clear message: *Why the fuck you asking me that dumbass question?*

The fellas weren't surprised at Byron's emphatic retort. They dragged on cigarettes, shuffled their feet, looked down at the dirt, gazed down the street to the west to see if customers were heading toward their drug spot, and listened to Bryon's final word on parenthood. "When I'm done fucking her, the rest is up to her."

Byron's pregnant girlfriend, Sylvia, probably didn't tell him that she had had sex with LaMont, Tyrone, DeShawn, Terrance, Andre, and Jamal in the past six months, that she didn't know which of those six young men was the baby's biological father, and that since she learned of her pregnancy during their relationship, she simply named Byron the baby daddy, the biological father.

Sylvia's designation of Byron as baby daddy did not invoke a biological father's legal responsibility. He wouldn't sign a birth certificate. There wouldn't be a paternity test. Byron publicly disavowed his role as progenitor and rejected any social or economic responsibility for the child the moment he heard Sylvia utter the words "I'm pregnant."

The Parole Officer

I taught a fall graduate course in criminal justice administration in the evening at the state university. There were only a dozen or so students each semester, and many were cops, probation officers, parole officers, and prison guards. They were bright, energetic, and fun to teach, and were always ready to tell good stories.

Brian was an adult parole officer who worked out of an office about fifty miles west of Bloomington. In class discussions he described his duties, the mounds of paperwork that kept him at his desk, and the hours each week he devoted to administrative tasks. He lamented the fact that he had relatively few days per week in the field to visit his adult parolee clients, who resided over a wide geographic area in central Illinois that included Champaign-Urbana. Brian and I laughed about the remote possibility that he might show up at a parolee's house and find the parolee chatting with me. We agreed that if we met in a parolee's house we'd pretend not to know each other.

Spring semester ended. I had no occasion to see Brian or any of the criminal justice professionals outside of class. A few years passed, I forgot about the possibility that Brian and I might in fact come face to face when he was on a parole visit.

Wednesday, late summer, about two in the afternoon, LaWanda, Trish, Sylvia, Ashanti, Harmony, Gracie, and Nilah and I were hanging out at Mario's. Lots of laughter, chatter, and gossiping were interrupted by a sound of car door slamming shut. Living room blinds were always closed. I lifted a slat, peeked out. Brian.

"Who's that?" LaWanda asked.

"I don't know, some guy carrying files," I responded.

"Shhh, keep quiet, it might be a parole officer."

A raucous room instantly fell dead silent. A friendly knock, Mario opened the door. Greetings were exchanged. Brian looked around the room. He saw me. His pupils opened wide. I detected a smirk. Mario introduced me as a teacher at the university, a friend of LaWanda's. Brian and I shook hands.

Brian asked Mario a few questions. "You looking for work?" "How do spend your days?" "How's your gramma?" Brian thanked Mario for trying his best to do the right thing. He acknowledged the young women sitting on the arms of chairs, leaning against walls and looking bored and annoyed at Brian's intrusion, and said he was glad to have met them. He nodded at me. "Nice to meet you, sir." Brian opened the door. Mario closed it.

Mario turned away from the door and toward the girls, who were beginning to make smirking noises, as they quietly told one another that Brian was a "silly ass motha fucker that oughta leave us alone."

The girls were about to break out laughing. Mario silenced them by putting his index finger on his lips. I stood up from the comfortable chair I had settled in when I arrived. I lifted a slat on beige aluminum front-window blind. Brian stopped at the driver's side door, unlocked it and turned toward the car to get inside. He glanced over his left shoulder, looked back at the house. He saw me peeking. He smiled, nodded. He drove away.

LaWanda's Moving Day

Soon after the Washington family moved into the White House, LaWanda decided to move into her own apartment. She dreamed of a blissful life with Mario and Mario Jr. in a tidy apartment in a quiet neighborhood. LaWanda grew up in a home with a mother and father and siblings, and she wanted that for her child too. LaWanda prepared for her move. Actually there was little to do. She had no furniture and only a small wardrobe. A spiffy Section 8 apartment awaited her arrival with Mario Jr. Her spot was located across the interstate in a quiet neighborhood where kids dropped their bikes and returned later to find them still lying in grass.

I drove LaWanda and Mario Jr. to their new digs, one of three adjacent apartments in a single-floor brick building. She opened the front door and expected to see furniture in her new home; instead, she faced an empty living room, two empty bedrooms, and an empty kitchen. Her eyes moistened. "What am I going to do?" I called the fixer, Burpee.

I drove LaWanda and Mario Jr. to a nearby fast-food joint, and shortly after we returned, Burpee's resolution to her problem arrived in the form of a small pickup loaded with furniture. Burpee supervised unloading. A young fellow and I lugged the living room furniture inside: a three-cushion blue couch; two matching single-cushion armchairs; a veneer coffee table just the right length to fit nicely in front of the couch. We hauled in two wooden tables to hold a lamp on each side of the couch.

Burpee's mission hadn't yet been accomplished. The truck was too small to haul everything. Off he went with his young driver, and soon they returned. The driver and I, again, lugged in mattresses, bed frames, a crib, a kid-sized bed, dressers, more lamps, and a Formica-top kitchen table with six chairs. When the furniture was delivered and properly positioned, Burpee the supervisor and the young fellow drove off. LaWanda had a nicely appointed home.

Iresha had told LaWanda's girlfriends about her move and soon after the furniture appeared, so did they. Young mothers and teenage girls filled the apartment, wandering about, cooing and rubbing and touching furniture. They tried out every piece of furniture, sat at the kitchen table, and even hopped up and down on the beds. The inevitable happened. Her friends posed a question I didn't want to hear. Where did LaWanda acquire such lovely new furniture? They wanted new furniture too. Who could blame them? These young mothers lived with shabby furniture, like the furniture in the White House. They looked at me like I was Santa Claus. At the moment when I thought I was going to have to conjure a plausible explanation to account for the new furniture, LaWanda's friends agreed by consensus that LaWanda would host a moving-in party.

The furniture looked brand new. Burpee had got his hands on goods that looked like the furniture college students used in dorm rooms and study rooms at Any State College. "Burp, where'd that furniture come from?," I inquired later at his house. He became indignant. "Don't you know better than to ask? Don't ask about anything that happens around here. Never ask a man where he got something. You'll get answers if you wait." I waited. No answers.

Moving-in Party

The news of LaWanda's moving-in party spread like a brush fire. By midafternoon Saturday, the day of the party, LaWanda's friends and their friends and their friends' friends had discovered the way to LaWanda's new apartment. A few of LaWanda's friends were friends with Iresha and her friends, Rebecca and Wizzy. Those girls were friends with Mikey and Shiba at the Pines. Mikey was friends with Dion and LaTola, whose friends were Johnnique, DeeDee, Kathy, and Claire. DeeDee hung out with Woozie and that opened the party to Derek, James, and Coolie. So it went.

LaWanda inhaled praise about the décor. Her friends and her friends' friends gushed over the new furniture. I'd seen the insides of the houses and apartments of people at the party. They didn't have new furniture. LaWanda was repeatedly asked, "Where'd you get this stuff?" Repeatedly, she said that her friends brought it over. Her friends said they wanted those kinds of friends.

The two-bedroom apartment was soon filled with teenagers and young men and women in their twenties standing shoulder to shoulder. The room was packed full of LaWanda's friends or a friend of a friend or a friend of a friend's friend. The kitchen, the master bedroom, the baby's room, the living room were filled with voices blending together into a crescendo of noise only reminiscent of human speech sounds. The music was played quietly, so that the new neighbors wouldn't be disturbed. Empty soda cans and bags of chips and popcorn filled plastic trash cans in the kitchen. Smoking was not permitted inside.

Loneliness

LaWanda was excited to move into her own spot. But when her apartment emptied and friends with children stopped coming by to hang out and let their children play together, reality hit. She was alone. She had dozens of friends. They all drifted away. No one came around; she passed the days by herself.

When the family lived at the Pines, the Blue House, the women's shelter, and the White House, LaWanda was surrounded by family and a continuous hustle and bustle. Iresha the social butterfly had friends coming and going at all hours. Memphis did grocery shopping for the family and prepared meals and made sure the home was as tidy and as peaceful as a home could be with three sons and two daughters. For twenty-one years at home LaWanda had been embraced by family and friends; now she awoke alone. She didn't have a car. Bus transportation was available if she was willing to walk about six blocks to the bus shelter. LaWanda wasn't a walker. Loneliness hurts.

The geographic distance between LaWanda and her family and friends produced a social distance. Her friends didn't have cars. Mo and Iresha didn't drive. Even if they had, there was no assurance they would drive three miles to visit LaWanda. LaWanda's Section 8 apartment, a wonderful idea, turned into a lonely reality. Then the hammer dropped. Brian appeared one day out of the blue and found Mario and his mates fogged over in a cloud of weed smoke. Having violated his parole, Mario was sent back to prison. I drove LaWanda and Mario Jr. back to the White House. Even after that bad experience of life on her own, she didn't give up on her fantasy of live-in bliss. Mario would learn his lesson this time, she asserted. Mario had an easy life on the street. Prison was even easier; out of sight, out of mind. Inside prison he didn't have to see or think about LaWanda and his son.

LaWanda's lifestyle, whether at the White House or on her own, was limited by her ability to earn an income. She lamented a continuous shortage of money. "Do you blame the white community for not helping you get a job?" "No," she answered. "It's my fault. I could have done better in school. I could have stayed in school. I didn't. It's my fault."

Value of Friends, Friends of Value

Friendships can be struck up when people's paths cross at home or school or in the neighborhood. The Washington family residence at the Pines, the Blue House, and the White House often looked like the train station downtown, with youngsters and adults coming and going at all hours. No surprise then that LaWanda's moving-in party brought girls together who hadn't seen each other for some time. Some in their early twenties had known each other since they were children. Some grew up together at the Pines or the Eastside Homes, another public housing project. By age twenty-five, it was common to find young women who had known one another ten or fifteen years.

On the north end, friendship meant more than someone to hang out with now and again. In their mid- to late teens, friends hung out all the time. Pregnancy and motherhood, however, interrupted hanging out. Some girls stopped seeing one another after they had children. Those who had children stopped seeing friends without children. Juicy accommodated her growing family by moving from the Pines five miles across town to the Eastside Homes. Motherhood and geographic distance separated and reduced the number of friends that girls had.

Young women had their favorite friends. Close or best friends were willing to share meals and babysitting duty and were willing to lend a hand if either friend got into serious trouble, like getting evicted from public housing for allowing a boyfriend to sell weed out of her apartment. That happened to Ericka, Nike's neighbor.

Ericka, age nineteen, had two children by two baby daddies. Coolie, her most recent boyfriend, who wasn't baby daddy to either of Ericka's children, came by to hang out. Soon Coolie encouraged Mut, Mike, and Country to stop by. They listened to music, smoked weed, and dished dime bags to weary travelers. Before long, Ericka's spot was holding all-night get-togethers. Music blasted and weed buyers traipsed around. Too many neighbors got annoyed. Someone called the cops. Neighbors watched the bust and laughed themselves silly, saying Ericka's guests slammed open the kitchen door and ran like the place was ablaze, while others busted out the apartment's front window, climbed through it, flopped down onto the wet grass, and ran off into the darkness. Ericka got evicted; drug selling on public housing property was strictly prohibited. Coolie, Mut, Mike, and Country disappeared as quickly as they had appeared the day they began invading Ericka's privacy.

Ericka's mama's spot across the grassy yard was too small to house Ericka and her children. Ericka's mama was taking care of Ericka's twenty-six-year-old sister's three preteen children, two boys and a girl, while Jamika did a sixty-month stint in prison, her third. Drugs. Ericka and her children moved and stayed with Juicy at the Eastside Homes until she was able to get her own apartment there. That's what friends do for one another.

Friendships create a social structure and patterns of interaction. Iresha has more than thirty friends; some are best friends, others are close friends, and still others are just friends. She hangs out more often and spends more time with best friends than close friends and friends. Still, they all are her friends, and she is their friend. Social closeness, feeling that you are best or close friends with some girls but not others creates social groups composed of young women who share different degrees of friendship.[4] Iresha's friends have their own friends, who have their own friends. Some of Iresha's friends are friends of one another, and some aren't. Friendships crisscross one another across the north end and beyond.

Braids Bind

Friday morning near 10, I parked in a lot at the Eastside Homes, about a quarter the size of the Pines. Sunshine leaked through spaces in the massive deciduous trees whose limbs kept the area cool on hot summer days. I enjoyed watching the Eastside Homes awaken, observing patterns of interaction among residents, as one friend and then another came outside, until the lawn filled with friends. Friday was the best day; it was hair-braiding day. Braids bind hair and bind people together.

When I pulled into the parking lot a youngster about age ten was tooling around on his bike, riding in circles to the left, then right, singing to himself and enjoying the warm weather and the chirping birds in early spring. I backed into a parking space near the dumpsters.

"Today a holiday?," I yelled at the bicyclist.

"Huh?" A blank look.

"Today a holiday?"

"No."

"No." I repeated. "Why aren't you in school?" He rode in circles, saying nothing. "Why aren't you in school?" I said, again.

"You a truant officer?"

"No. I'm a teacher. Why aren't you in school?" I smiled. He explained that his mother didn't wake up early enough to wake him.

"No one cares if I go to school."

Soon after I arrived, Felicia, age twenty-nine, and her daughters, Heather, age twelve, and Keona, age ten, headed out to buy groceries. They yelled "Hi," waved at me, said they'd be back soon.

Around 10:30, Tina and Rebecca, a mother and daughter ages thirty-five and sixteen, ambled out of their apartment carrying two kitchen chairs, a wooden table, and a boom box.

I knew they wouldn't disappoint. It was braiding day, a social occasion girls and boys and men and women enjoyed on Friday morning in warm weather. Preparations were underway. The weekend beckoned.

Kiy came out about fifteen minutes later. She'd spent the night with Monike, though she usually stays a few miles west of the Pines. Tina had started on Rebecca's hair. Kiy and Monike waited.

Folks came to wait, listen to music, gossip, share secrets, smoke a blunt. Kiy yelled at me. She told me not to be shy. Join the party. I moseyed over. She smiled at me, said someone would braid my hair if I had hair. Laughter all around.

Maurice and PeeWee soon joined the party. They needed their hair done too. By this time, several more kitchen chairs dotted the lawn. PeeWee jumped in one before someone else took it. Another car drove up, parked. Ernest drove in. Don rode shotgun. Henry was hanging out the back window, yelling, "Anybody got a blunt?"

About 12:30 Keona and her girls returned. Coria, Keona's mama, had joined them. Together they carried bag after bag after bag of groceries into Keona's apartment at the east end of the northern-most row of apartments. Grocery bags stored away inside, Keona and Heather came out again, yelled "Hi" to everyone. Everyone said "Hi" back, waving their arms and gesturing "Come over here," encouraging them to join the fun. Keona declined. She and Heather walked back to the car. It looked like a 1970-ish Fairlane, dented, rusted. Duct tape held a tail light in place. Where the passenger-side rear window should have been, there was an empty space covered with hazy heavy-duty plastic taped on its edges to the window opening.

Keona grabbed and opened the trunk lid. She and Heather dug around, lifted out two cases of cooking oil, four gallons per box. They struggled while walking and talking and laughing on their way back to the apartment. I sat on the grass watching them haul oil. I was eager to see if any of the half-dozen strapping young men sitting shirtless on the grass would volunteer to exercise their muscles, relieving Keona and Heather of their oil-carting task. Fellas didn't budge. Hauling oil like rearing kids, that's women's work.

Two days later, Sunday, I stopped by Keona's just to say hi. Truthfully, I was nosey. I was curious about the groceries they had bought. Grocery shopping entailed harvesting all manner of greasy, fat-laden, high-calorie, artery-clogging, belly-busting boxed, bagged, or wrapped consumables. Vegetables, fruits, and cereals like oatmeal were either overlooked or sold out in a jiffy after hitting shelves in local groceries.

Standing over the four-burner electric stove, a guy in his early twenties heated a quart saucepan filled to the brim with cooking oil. When the oil smoked, he dropped pieces of frozen breaded shrimp encrusted with ice particles into the bubbling oil, just like Memphis did that night I met Jason. Hot oil droplets flew out of the pan. He cooked those breaded shrimp long enough to have deep-fried a turkey. He lifted a slotted metal spoon with a broken black plastic handle exposing thin metal off the counter and was about to dip it into an erupting pan of hot oil, which I knew from experience would quickly heat the handle red hot. The budding chef, just about to fry his palm and fingers, listened to me when I said, "Put a towel on the metal, you'll burn yourself." He nodded thanks. He scooped out the pieces of burned, encrusted shrimp. He remembered to turn off the burner. Then, holding a towel, he reached out to grab the blistering hot pan, oil droplets still settling down to a calm boil. He lifted the pan off the stove, turned to place it into a wet metal sink with a faucet leaking drops of water. I hinted that he might not want to put a pan of boiling oil into a wet sink with a dripping faucet. I explained that oil and water don't mix, that hot oil would fly up if water hit it, badly scaling him. He nodded again. He offered me a piece of shrimp. "No, thanks," although it was a generous gesture.

7

Rebirth Days

The story of Burpee's birth sounds like the mythic birth of a Greek hero.

On a cold and dark wintry night on Chicago's north side, sometime in the 1950s, Burpee's father hailed a cab. His mother, already in the late stages of labor, crawled onto the back seat. They sped off in the direction of a public hospital, but traffic and harsh weather slowed the cab. The labor of child-birth, meanwhile, progressed quickly. Burpee's mother yelled at the driver to stop. Winds whipped around blowing icy rain and snow. The driver pulled over and stopped under the elevated train, where he found a bit of protection. The driver opened the back door on his side of the car and reached toward Burpee's mother. People gathered around, shoving one another toward the cab's open back door, crowding together to watch the birth. A baby boy arrived on a cold, wintry, and stormy night. His mother named him Burpee, in honor of the cabbie who delivered him.

Chronological age measures the progress of life in years. Burpee's mother didn't have a birth certificate. When we met in 1996, he said he was fifty-two. Who knows? A less popular measure of time counts the number of stints a person has been incarcerated in a juvenile detention facility, a jail, or a prison. His heroin-clouded memory didn't recall with certainty the number of times he went to juvenile detention and jail, but he did remember the number of times he had been released from prison.

We met ten months after his sixth release. He considered each prison release a rebirth day. His first five rebirth days didn't turn out too well. So, he celebrated only his sixth rebirth day. Burpee didn't attribute religious meaning to rebirth days, although the symbolic imagery of a prison giving birth to an innocent seems compelling. Actually though, Burpee the Innocent seems a bit excessive.

Burpee crawled out of the depths of Chicago's juvenile hall in the 1950s. His memories of juvenile detention and jail included bare-knuckle fighting bouts that determined inmates' pecking order. Although he didn't tell me why his mother was imprisoned, he did say that she was the most outrageous criminal in a family of criminals. His brothers and sisters did time; he wouldn't talk about them. His father ran a numbers racket. He did time too. Several extended family members did time on Illinois's death row. He didn't want to talk about them or their offenses. The Illinois governor mandated a moratorium on executions in the late 1990s. Death sentences were commuted to life without parole. To say Burpee was gleeful at hearing the news would be an understatement.

Crystal, a beautiful baby girl whose mother was Burpee's eleventh baby mama, joined the Burpee family in the mid-1990s. As well as we could determine, the births of some of his children corresponded more or less to about nine months after the time he was back on the street between stints in prison. His first ten children's names derived from a Burp paradigm. Burp-A, his eldest son, a violent career criminal, was his pride and joy. His other children, male and female, were named in alphabetic sequence, Burp-B, Burp-C, and so on. Crystal was the exception.

I didn't meet Burp-A through Burp-J. Burp-A shadowed in his daddy's footsteps and achieved notoriety as a high-ranking member of the Four Corner Hustlers (FCH) on Chicago's north side. Although I asked repeatedly, Burpee didn't explain what it meant to be a high-ranking FCH member or what Burp-A did to achieve that rank. I was about to learn.

While watching CNN and chatting in his living room about his success at impeding a state prison gang riot, Burpee stopped midsentence, stood up, rambled to the television, grabbed a copy of Burp-A's wanted poster off the top, which, he said, was on display at that time in Chicago police stations on the north side. Someone copied and faxed the wanted poster to him, a family album kind of thing. The wanted poster alleged that Burp-A was violent, armed, and extremely dangerous, all characteristics Burpee felt were worthy of his pride. When he stared at the wanted poster, his face exuded the particular pleasure a father experiences when his son successfully follows in his footsteps.

After I moved to Cleveland in 2002, Burpee and I chatted by phone now and then. He called the first time to tell me the FBI nabbed Burp-A on a racketeer influenced and corrupt organization (RICO) indictment. A guilty verdict in Chicago's federal district court sentenced Burp-A to 120 months in federal prison. He called a second time to ask about federal sentencing guidelines. He wanted specific information about federal prisoner designation procedures.[1] There were two medium-security federal correctional institutions (FCI) in Illinois. FCI, Pekin, was located about an hour west of Bloomington. FCI, Greenville, was located near East St. Louis, Illinois. Burpee wanted to visit Burp-A and asked if there was anything he could do to get Burp-A designated to one facility rather than the other.

Attorneys generally don't know the specifics of federal prison policies. I told Burpee what he needed to know about inmate designation and suggested he pass along the information to Burp-A's attorney. If Burp-A had his father's temperament, he wouldn't slide easily into a federal prison routine. To help out, I gave Burpee a list of recommendations on the proper defendant decorum in federal courts and in federal prisons to pass on to Burp-A, offering a list of prisoner dos and don'ts. Burpee told me repeatedly that Burp-A did enjoy inflicting violent harm on folks who pissed him off. Like father, like son. Burpee listened intently when I told him that if Burp-A acted aggressively toward a federal prison staff member, shanked a fellow prisoner, was caught having sex with an inmate or staff member, or abandoned self-control and told a federal warden to "go fuck him- or herself," he would most definitely spend at least a number of months measured in triple digits at the high-security penitentiary in Colorado. I recommended that Burpee tell Burp-A that even though he'd enjoy the view of Pike's Peak from the federal penitentiary's recreation yard, he'd be far better off abiding by the rules while serving a seemingly never ending number of months in federal prison.

Matthew 6:13

Burpee's survival of his criminal adventures, stories about which he aired with pride, demonstrated a degree of mental and physical strength sufficient to pull him through decades of trials and tribulations. Burpee thought of himself as a convict's convict, a man of tough body and tough mind. Ex-convicts like Burpee, Alabama, Cliff, and Jaboo often say "Street's hard, prison's easy," which is a verbal acknowledgment that their hard-headed stick-to-itiveness has enabled them to overcome whatever the streets tossed their way. Prison is the easy way out. Doing time came as a welcome relief. "Going to the joint ain't nothing des' days," Burpee said. "It don' take a man to do time no more. Dudes lay up in they bunks, watch color television, HBO, and get whatever a man need. Back in my day, a dude had to fight to stay alive. I had to kill a dude once a week just to keep up my rep." Killing to keep up his rep was a favorite line practiced repeatedly to my students and on occasion colleagues who visited me and wanted to meet him.

Burpee avoided the temptation to reengage in avocations at which he was a journeyman, like drug dealing and strong-arming the weak, which were easy ways off the street, a path to an easier life inside prison. Cliff and Tracy took that easy path. Burpee stayed out of trouble after his sixth release, and the reasons for it can be debated in the jargon of criminological or sociological theories, but it's easier to explain his straight life in plain English. He enjoyed his life and his family and now his freedom. He was respected. He had friends. He seemed happy and satisfied. He helped folks like LaWanda and felt needed and appreciated. He earned money the old-fashioned way: he worked for it. He had what I had—a job, a family, some friends, a home, and a reason to look forward to tomorrow.

When he was released the sixth time, he had maxed out his sentence, meaning he had served all of it and so had no parole time. It wasn't the threat of a new charge, a new prison term, that kept him straight. He thrived on talking about the hustle, the conniving, the backroom deals. It excited him to remind me of his ability to strong-arm folks into doing things his way, merely by reminding them of his street reputation. I didn't see him connive or strong-arm anyone. He relished his back-in-the-day stories, tales of running the streets, gangbanging, hustling dope, conniving straights into buying street insurance, the street criminal's version of the glory days, high-school football, cheer-leaders, big man on campus.

No matter what he told me about his life on the streets, fact or fiction, exaggerations or outright lies, scars on his arms and back recorded a history of violence and addiction. Burpee didn't wear short-sleeve shirts. Now and then I spotted his lower forearms through the oblong space that opened when he secured the wrist button on long-sleeve shirts. Long after we met, he pointed out heroin tracks running up and down both forearms and scars left by infected abscesses. He recounted tales of bullet-wound scars and knife-fight scars on his upper body, chest, and back.

The scars were a record of ugliness in his life story. At the time I met him, I thought that being his fifties, he must be tired of running the streets and way too weary to fight for more scars. But those are clichés, easy explanations. He had energy aplenty. I watched him respond in foul ways when people threatened him or his baby girl Crystal. He re-fused to succumb to temptations such as skimming the income of local drug sellers—so easy, so profitable—that carried the inevitable risk of arrest and imprisonment, which would put distance between him and Crystal.

Burpee cherished his story. It brought him praise. It was mythic. He arose out of Chicago slums. He stayed strong. He beat back proverbial dragons. He endured. On the north end he found the holy grail: respect accorded him by his community. He succeeded in his community. There, on the north end, he invested time and effort to keep men like Alabama strong and on the street.

On the north end, he wasn't a pariah, an outcast, an ex-con people didn't want in their backyard. He wasn't feared, scorned, ridiculed, ignored, shoved aside, and disrespected by his community. There, in his community, he was known as a strong man, a provider for his family, a loving father, and a man who freely gave his time and energy to others. He achieved a balance between needing praise and doing good deeds for which he received praise. In his absence, no one would have moved LaWanda. No one would have watched over Alabama. No one would have kept a vigil on youngsters on the edge of falling into street life. He didn't want them to become the tough guy they thought was cool. He kept kids on the straight and narrow with just a stern facial expression and a few well-chosen words.

Burpee didn't ask to be respected in mainstream culture. Out there in the world dominated by well-educated free men and women, he was the best example of how everything can go wrong in a person's life. He was the archetype of criminological risk factors. In the mainstream world he was disregarded and pushed aside. He was a guy the world of free men and women wanted to transform into their own image of a reformed criminal. In his world, in his culture, he had respect. No one looked askance at his six prison terms, addictions, and criminal record. In his culture there were no faceless jurists of moral behavior.

I invited him often to lecture in my university classes. Burpee's quick sense of humor and sharp tongue engaged undergraduate and graduate students. Before my eyes, he transformed from public jokester into gangster, then into preacher, then into parent, and then back into public jokester. Gangster Burpee's speech hardened, it oozed out slowly in a staccato, choppy flow of street talk, and his posture stiffened into a fighting pose. Gangster Burpee hopped off the FBI's most wanted list and appeared in front of student audiences. He adored the spotlight. He fancied his ability to terrify college students. Students' evaluations reported that over a long semester he was the best part of the course. Burpee the ex-convict gangster appeared in living color as a mythic character.

Doting Dad

Burpee's house was his "spot." Folks drove by, slowed and beeped, waved, or stopped to chat and check out an odd sight, a white man chatting with Burpee at his home. His next-door neighbors occasionally joined him outside. Together they all watched Crystal play. When she played outside, he wasn't fearful that she'd toddle off the grass onto the sidewalk or into the street. An anchor fence encircled his grassy lawn. He hovered nearby, never leaving her alone, never letting her out of his sight. Burpee's gentle fathering attested to his rich emotional attachment. He caressed Crystal with warmth and tenderness, smiled while she played, talked quietly to her, and when he held her, his eyes glimmered like moonlight bouncing off iced snowdrifts.

Crystal attended a religious preschool. A school bus arrived daily. Daddy Burpee held her hand and guided her up steps too steep for tiny legs. When she walked down the central aisle, we could barely see the top of her head. Burpee didn't move away until he saw her find a seat. She sat on the sidewalk side of the bus, always the side closest to her dad. He waved goodbye. She waved. He threw a kiss.

A short time before I moved away in 2002, he told me his wife was pregnant again. When I heard that Crystal would soon be a big sister, I asked, "You're not going to name the baby Burp-L, are you?" The birth of Crystal's brother or sister meant that Burpee would have two children with the same baby mama, a first worth noting.

Burpee's Eleventh Baby Mama

A long time passed before I could piece together snippets of the story of Burpee and Crystal's mama. Whether he didn't want to talk about her or didn't want to think about her or couldn't remember parts of their history, I didn't know. When I did ask about their relationship, he usually looked at me through squinty eyes that I took to mean "stop bothering me with all these questions." I stopped asking questions and just listened.

Burpee and Latisha weren't legally married. Referring to themselves as married in public settings legitimized their relationship and his daughter. He wanted Crystal's teachers, friends, and folks at school to think of her mom and dad as citizens.

Latisha was a Gangster Disciple (GD), a member of a local family with kinship roots on Chicago's south side. Some members of her family remained there. Others had moved to the north end at some time no one could pinpoint.

Burpee said several north end families like Latisha's were gang families; that is, families in which multiple generations were affiliated with the same gang. To learn what it meant to be born into a gang family,

I asked Joyce, an eighteen-year-old GD whom I'd known for several years.

"At what age did you join a gang?"

"Six," she replied.

I challenged her. "Six, that's a bit too young to join a gang, don't you think?"

"I was born into it," she explained.

Relatives in her parents' generation and her cousins were GDs, she said. I asked her to account for them. "Where do they live?" "How old are they?" "Have any been to prison?" She didn't have answers. Joyce had a part-time job, attended community college, had no criminal history and no arrests. I suspected, though I couldn't verify it, that tales of north end gang families were family folklore, akin to Big C's status as a three-star Vice Lord, or gangsters sniping at cop cars, or the north end's reputation as too dangerous to drive through if you're white. Stories like these are a type of family property, a way to attach distinctive characteristics to a social group, such as a multigenerational family, in a community as culturally and economically homogeneous as the north end.[2]

Burpee met Latisha on the north end. She was "deep into it [gang life]," he said. He told me she had a few bullet wounds to prove it. I didn't see those scars. Those wounds, he said, had been inflicted decades earlier.

Like couples occasionally do, she and Burpee had knock-down, drag-out verbal bouts. He never hit her. I wondered if he controlled his temper out of respect for his baby mama or fear that her relatives would gun him down or whether he considered hitting a woman a sign of weakness. I didn't ask. Intimate partner violence on the north end wasn't common, as far as I knew. I didn't witness intimate partner violence or see bruises that came with hitting nor did I hear males telling tales of "whuppin'" girlfriends.

The folklore of gang families on the north end has historical roots. Years earlier at a time no one clearly remembered, Burpee's Black Gangster Disciples (BGD) had a prominent place on the north end. BGDs and GDs got into it, Burpee said. BGDs broke into a GD drug house, intending to rip off drugs and cash. Latisha, then a teenager, had been shot during the break-in. He didn't know if he had shot her or one of his boys had. As a footnote he added that it didn't matter who shot her. The rest of the story seems lost in the fog of gun smoke and enveloped Burpee family folklore. Time passed. Latisha and Burpee lived together several times, but each try at domestic bliss ended in disaster. Eventually, their daughter Crystal brought them together once again, giving them yet one more shot at domestic bliss. When I moved away in 2002, Burpee and his wife had been living together since I had arrived on the north end in 1996.

Protecting Kin

Burpee protected the people he cared about, and among those Crystal was first and foremost. She enjoyed playing outdoors on warm evenings after dusk. However, a house across the street — only about thirty yards from his — was a drug spot. That juxtaposition, a drug house on one side of the street and Crystal nearby on the other side, provoked anger that he normally hid away out of public view. That drug spot threatened Crystal. It threatened him.

Burpee watched Crystal play while we chatted with neighbors. He loved his built-in audience. While laughing and retelling the same stories over and over, night by night, all of a sudden he'd stop talking, stare across the street, drift off into a dark place, and then return to finish his stories. The look in his eyes, a look I hadn't seen before, was ominous.

"What's up with that spot across the street? I never see anybody go in or out during the day." I goaded him with a dumb question.

"What's it look like, Joe? Shades down all the time. People going in and out all night long. What's wrong wid ju man?" Burpee called me Joe once in a while, sometimes when we were hanging out and laughing, other times when he got pissed off at something, like that drug spot. One day, out of the blue, he said he wanted to buy that house.

"So what's up with that house, Burp? You really want to buy it?"

"I ain't gonna buy it. What's wrong with you? Me and some boys are going over there soon. I'll make 'em a deal." His godfather persona.

"A deal?" I probed, making it sound like I didn't know what sort of deal he'd offer.

"Yeah, Joe, a deal. They gonna walk out or get carried out." Sounded like something I didn't want to know about or watch.

I got busy tracking down north end folks and doing interviews and working at home on data I'd been gathering on the north end. I hadn't seen Burpee in about a week. I drove by his spot. If I didn't see his Caddy, I would keep driving. But I saw the Caddy, so I parked in front of his house. Crystal was playing outside.

"Is your daddy here?" She smiled and pointed across the street at the house.

I walked across the street. Windows had been removed. Doors had been taken off hinges. I walked in. His boys had the floor ripped open. Hammers were banging, power saws were screaming, rebuilding was underway.

"What are you going to do with this place?"

"I'm gonna live here."

"Why? You got a house." I pointed across the street. He paused. Then I heard the tale of his tumultuous marriage, its ups and downs, mostly downs. He needed breathing space, a place to go when things got bad.

I missed the real estate deal. Burpee and his boys brokered the deal in the dead of night. Closing on the house might have involved weapons, threats, and the infliction of bruises. I knew it was best that I hadn't been there and that I didn't ask questions now about Burpee's mode of acquisition. The prospect of a subpoena ordering me to court to testify against Burpee in a criminal case, frankly, made me nauseous. If an ethnographer hangs around a long time, he or she sees and hears a lot. In a litigious society such as ours, I couldn't risk seeing serious wrongdoing so that someone who saw me could proffer my name in a plea agreement or benefit if I weren't able to testify. I didn't want to end up in the local obits.

Burpee kept his word. He acquired the house across the street. He bought it, so he claimed. The price was astonishingly low, well below market value. I never learned the exact price. When I brought it up, he'd ignore me. "Just keep driving, Joe. You don't wanna know." Amen.

Rebirth Day

Like every experienced street hustler I had ever seen, Burpee's tone of voice, body posture, and, when necessary, his evil eye controlled social interactions.

Six times prison gates rolled back releasing Burpee, a free man yet again. His first five release days didn't rewind the clock or create a fresh start, but on the date of his sixth release we celebrated at his favorite restaurant, Burger King. We strolled in together, then he charged to the counter like he was about to rob the joint, turned on the evil eye, leaned flat onto the counter, and stared up at the menu. The young man behind the counter watched him, a bit scared, a bit puzzled at the sight of a squirrely old man glaring up at him. Burpee pulled himself up, leaned on his elbows, and snarled, "You give senior citizen discounts, don't you?"

We ate at Burger King on release day (and on many others day, too), and he'd always repeat his senior citizen discount act, a fun sight to watch. I always felt sorry for the scared counter kids. Burpee was compulsive. We had to eat at the same Burger King location every time; no other location would do.

Burpee refused to carry folding money—I had no idea if he had any cash and didn't ask—and he had no credit cards, of course. I financed celebrations and ordinary meals. I was the white man with the money, after all. At the first release day celebration, before I knew that Burpee's rules of fast food ordering required that I pay the tab, he liked to say, "We get what we're owed." Silly me; I really felt like I owed him more than fast-food meals.

Citizen Burpee

Burpee was alive with laughter and stories of yesterday and was able to broadcast hope for the future of men and women sequestered in state prisons, hopeful that after release these men would join his flock of ex-cons at Homey Hills. Out of sight, off the streets, tucked away in apartments and houses on the north end were men who had been released from state prisons and were employed in indoor jobs, outside public view and shielded from the condemnation of the outside world that comes with the moniker "convicted felon." Those men got their start at Homey Hills. Burpee smoothed ex-cons' way back into straight life. He was the ex-con go-between who came to the aid of guys new on the street in need of employment, men like Alabama.

Burpee hired ex-cons for his boiler room if he thought they could stay straight, clean, and sober and not raise hell. Ex-cons needed only reading ability for this job. After a few days practicing the phone script, they were on the payroll. Off-hours, he derived pleasure by acting as the north end's unofficial community outreach social worker, helping young women like LaWanda at my behest and coaxing teenage fellas to mow lawns in the summer instead of pitching weed.

Burpee was a citizen, Pastor Burpee, a straight guy running a good-guy hustle. The term "ex-con" seems to elicit an automatic response in mainstream citizens, who are wary and back off and can't wait to turn and run away. That's a reasonable response. Men like the mountain-sized Alabama or the gun-wielding, strong-arm robber called Crazy Eye or the slick-talking drug hustler Jaboo had criminal records that proved they had once been dangerous men. But with Burpee's help, they got jobs and went to work every day. Alabama even had a girlfriend he married after a few straight years on the street. Jaboo and Crazy Eye had people on the north end they stayed with, folks they cared about who cared about them. Burpee hired sex offenders, too. The boiler room kept them out of sight and out of the community's mind.

Burpee's ex-con employees enjoyed the workplace. The repetitive job, reciting the same script over and over, seemed to me to be a down-right bore. His workers seemed content with what I considered utterly tedious, mind-numbing work. But ex-cons know how to cope with repetition, how not to watch the clock. Over years or decades in prison, inmates fill thousands of hours huddling over checker and chess boards and dominos tables. On a nameless day—all days are alike inside prison—inmates hang out in the yard, walk clockwise circles around a track, do pull-ups and lift barbells, and then do those things again on the next nameless day. Inmates mill around dorms and cell blocks, watch television, play cards, and lean against walls, talking endlessly.

Serving a prison sentence of ten years boils down to repeating one day thousands of times, just like reading a script day after day in the boiler room. Ex-cons do tomorrow what they did today, and they know well that it's useless to complain about anything. Prisons don't have happy hour.

Burpee's pastor persona neutralized citizens' fear. There was no need for him to admit to his past criminality or to his decades of doing prison time. He kept that dark backstage life hidden as well as he could. I knew what lurked behind the curtain of civility, and I thought that a lifelong criminal like Burpee doing good deeds for the right reasons was as likely as finding the pea in three-card molly. I waited for the ax to fall. I thought he must skim off private donations to Homey Hills or quietly twist the arms of ex-cons, conning them to "donate" a bit of their paychecks earned in legit jobs downtown back to Homey Hills, allegedly to cut the cost of their per diem. With skim and kickbacks he could have earned a decent income. I was surprised, then, that he didn't appear to skim or twist arms or con anyone. I didn't see material evidence that his income increased in an unusual way over the years we spent together. He wore the same clothes over and over; he drove the same rundown Caddy with ripped seams on front seats, year after year. I still paid the bill on release day celebrations.

Homey Hills

Homey Hills ran smoothly. The final time I was there, about three dozen ex-cons were assembled: drug dealers, armed robbers, burglars, gangbangers, and strong-arm street thugs who ripped off drug dealers among other miscreants that civilians did not want in their neighborhoods. The facility's grounds were enclosed by an eight-foot-high anchor fence (no razor wire) and a locked exit gate. Men entered and exited through a remodeled building, which included a dining room, a chapel, offices, and a desk at which they checked in and out.

Homey Hills brought about a striking role reversal: Burpee enforced the rules of a daily routine like a warden. Burpee the warden had the fellas up early. They attended breakfast and a religious service, then caught a bus to downtown jobs or worked on the property, refurbishing motel rooms. Men learned trades by seeing and doing and were instructed by journeymen tradesmen: plumbers, electricians, carpenters, painters, and carpet installers.[3] At the end of the work day, men attended another religious service, ate dinner, and participated in group therapy. No alcohol. No drugs. No crime. No smoking. No sex. In Warden Burpee's halfway house there were no second chances. If men chose to violate Homey Hills' prerelease rules, they had to live with the consequences.

Burpee had no magic formula, no sure-fire, six-week prerelease program with therapeutic aftercare that transformed players into citizens. He smoothed ex-cons' way back into straight life by understanding where they had come from, what they had done, and what they faced when the gates rolled back. Homey Hills operated on a strict schedule, enforced by a man who'd been inside six times, had a long criminal record, and had stayed out of prison after his sixth release. Ex-cons at Homey Hills respected him and knew he enforced the rules without exception. No wiggle room. No excuses. No second chances.

Burpee's Path to Redemption

Burpee didn't have a strategic plan, a detailed programmatic design, an implementation strategy, or measures of success. There was only one measure of success at Homey Hills, he said: not violating its rules. Over our time together, bits and pieces of the rationale that he used to structure Homey Hills emerged in casual conversations. Burpee's thoughts on Homey Hills' rigid rules were mindful of the fact that prison's easy and the street's hard, that ex-cons had to learn how to live on the streets like they had to learn how to live in prison and that, like addicts, ex-cons fail and try again and again until they learn how to stay straight.

Street hustlers have no responsibility to anyone but themselves. They don't want or don't know how to live a straight life. They don't wear a watch or heed time schedules. If everything goes wrong, as it had for Burpee six times, prisons rescue hustlers. Street life poses a daily struggle and continuous threats to personal safety and does not give freely of a safe place to sleep or food to eat. Prison life eliminates the ambiguities of street life; men get in prison those things they struggled for and failed to get on the street. Life in prison, however, comes at a cost: personal freedom. But this cost is a small price to pay if players have no money. Burpee insisted, "If you got no money, you got no freedom."

Burpee intuitively understood what it meant to be raised on the streets, abandoned and alone like Wooch, a boy no one worried about when it was cold and dark. Men like Wooch were raised on the street; they dropped out of school, were rarely employed in straight jobs, wouldn't sit in classrooms, wouldn't abide by rules, didn't learn how to be punctilious. The consequence was a semiliterate, rule-breaking, obstreperous teenager no one wanted.

Prisons have an open-door policy and welcome everyone, teaching them how to live by a strict schedule, a schedule no different from that followed by men and women who catch a train at 6:34 in the morning, arrive at work by 7:30, eat lunch between 11:15 and 11:45, attend meetings at 1:30, 2:15, and 3:45 in the afternoon, dash to Central Station to catch the 5:14 train back to the suburbs, and then repeat that schedule the next day, the next month, the next year, until they are released and enjoy retirement.

Within the structure of prison life inmates have leeway to do as they please, over lunch break, work breaks, and evening hours. There is recreation, hobby shop, and religious get-togethers, or inmates simply hang out, like they did back in the day on the north end. Prison life comes with a built-in social life. Street partners, family members, friends, and guys from down the block regroup in prison.

In that social milieu inmates garner a sense of personal identity. Burpee called himself a "convict" and jokingly referred to himself as "booty bandit."[4] A convict is a tough guy who can't be bullied, abides by his own rules and others' only by necessity, and never sides with prison staff. "Stand-up" cons like him are known, recognized, and respected. Over time a convict's prison persona emerges. When released convicts bring that prison persona to the streets, there's trouble. Each time Burpee played out his convict persona on the street, he returned to prison.

Burpee held that when the gates roll back, the structure of daily prison life, the ease of prison social life, the built-in amusements of prison daily routines like checkers and chess games, and the necessities prison provides like a clean place to sleep and daily meals all immediately disappear, and the disappearance of these built-in comforts has traumatic effects. The instant the prison gates slam shut behind the ex-cons, they are locked out of the life they had had over years or decades. Ex-cons, Burpee argued, needed a prison corollary, a daily life that was a gentler version of the life men had inside. That corollary was Homey Hills, where over time and among men like themselves, paroled inmates could learn to drop their convict persona and find another persona that worked to their advantage outside prison.

Doing the Right Thing

The street's tough. The trick to staying on the street was getting the right job among the right people.[5] Burpee's workers got a paycheck. Their financial reward helped out. Their personal reward, feeling satisfied at work, came with regaining what they had lost when they walked away from prison. They regained camaraderie and an intuitive familiarity, knowing that everyone on the job had similar criminal and prison experiences, facilitated by prison humor, tall tales, and laughter. Polished hustlers and storytellers fill prison cell blocks. These guys, like Burpee, adore an audience who will listen to tall tales that are trumped up, twisted, exaggerated, entertaining stories of a raucous and wild criminal lifestyle when they did what they wanted to do with impunity, denying personal responsibility for the pain inflicted on their victims, except when they lied to a sentencing judge about having feelings of remorse.

Burpee told me that in black neighborhoods people do their business in the street. If men who had done time intended to get a job and stay working, Burpee explained, they felt comfortable living near and working around people like themselves. Take Alonzo, for example.

The north end was safe for Alonzo. He had been inside many times and had been straight for more than ten years when we met. Alonzo fixed cars on his dirt driveway or along the curb on the street in front of his house. His customers had done time. He was proud of staying straight, though he didn't like talking about the days of running the streets in Chicago. Those days were long over. His proudest accomplishment, he said with glow in his eyes, was his daughter, who had finished a master's degree at the nearby university. I didn't confirm that claim. Fact or folklore, at least he wasn't thinking about drugs and robbery. He enjoyed talking about his daughter and trying to convince me to let him do mechanical work on my Passat.

Men like Crazy Eye, Jaboo, and Alabama walk forever in the dark shadow cast by prison. Recovery comes over several months after their release, when they have lost the look of time travelers stunned by sights they had never seen, like an ATM or even a touch-tone landline phone. Five, ten, twenty years inside a prison and then one day, bang, a gate slides behind them, locking them away from a world they know well, people they know, and things they enjoy. They are free men. They walk into a world, alone, wandering aimlessly like Cliff did or suffering an unsatisfied compulsion to shoot heroin or smoke a rock pipe or knock back a forty. Then along comes Burpee.

The Convict and the Professor

Over five decades, the fuel that fed Burpee's anger sluggishly diminished. Burpee ran a straight hustle and did it well. He earned praise and community-wide recognition, a voice at the proverbial table with local law enforcement personnel who patrolled the north end and a voice in my university classrooms. On a local stage he earned respect. I thought he had earned and deserved access to a stage bigger than the north end. I spoke to colleagues at the Illinois attorney general's Gang Crime Prevention Center. They agreed to meet him. I had talked about Burpee so often to Professor Spergel that he wanted to meet him. I had a plan in mind to improve Burpee's way of life. Unfortunately I didn't remember that he was a hustler, a player who'd go along as long as there was a reward in the end. In this instance, the reward he had in mind was the short-lived limelight and applause for a life of crime, gangbanging, and slinging dope. Burpee the star.

Burpee and I drove to visit Spergel at the University of Chicago and then we dodged our way around downtown traffic and headed toward the Gang Crime Prevention Center. When we arrived in Chicago and before we drove south to Hyde Park, Burpee insisted on visiting a neighborhood he called "Jew Town."

Jew Town was a thriving neighborhood back in the day, a place where merchants sold clothing at low prices. Little did I know at that moment, but it also was the place where he had hustled. In his younger days, he disclosed in an uncharacteristically quiet voice, he ran the streets in Jew Town, though he refused to tell me what he did there.

The Jews of Jew Town were gone. In its place was a devastated, albeit energized, neighborhood, home to impoverished black residents. A sidewalk jazz group played. Grills and smokers filled the air with sweet smells of food for sale. Kids ran among the cars at stoplights, pitching packages of white socks, like impoverished and homeless boys and girls I had seen trying to sell packages of socks, running dangerously among slowly moving cars on Istanbul's jammed-up streets. Burpee's memory of Jew Town didn't comport with a neighborhood so battered it looked like black and white films of European cities bombed at the end of World War II. He scrunched his face in disappointment as we drove south to Hyde Park and the majesty and manicured grounds of the University of Chicago.

We drove south on Lake Shore Drive along Lake Michigan, exited and zipped past the Museum of Science and Industry, and in a few blocks, we were on campus. Burpee smiled and laughed when he saw the expansive greenery on the university's Midway Plaisance. It reminded him of a prison's big yard, he noted, without razor wire and guard towers.

We browsed campus, stopped at the cafeteria adjacent to the book-store, and walked the campus perimeter. We walked to the corner of the Midway at the intersection of East 60th Street and South Cottage Grove Avenue, the southwest edge of the campus. Across the street, a few hundred feet away, was one of Chicago's most violent neighbor-hoods, according to Professor Spergel, separated by a city street from the campus. I couldn't resist a bit of anthropology talk and broke into an explanation of the concepts of social areas and cultural spaces. No walls, no razor wire–topped fences, and no walking police patrols kept south side gangbangers away from the Midway. A city street separated these two cultural and social areas like a barrier of bubbles in an aquar-ium separates sharks and bait fish.

We arrived at Spergel's research office. I introduced Burpee to the professor. Instant rapport. They chatted and laughed like old friends or cellmates. Spergel paid attention and listened to Burpee explain that millions were wasted on gang prevention and intervention and that with a dozen old lawn mowers and a few hundreds for gas money, he'd "put dem shorties out on the streets, working, cutting grass, . . . working all day, getting too tired to [gang] bang." Just as the debate was about to move into a higher gear, it was interrupted by the professor's ringing phone and his research assistants knocking at his office door wanting to meet Burpee, whom the professor introduced as an "OG" (original gangster), "a Black Gangster Disciple."

They got along famously, the gangster and the professor. We enjoyed lunch in the faculty dining room, and then it was time to go. Professor Spergel invited him back any time. Burpee inflated like a hot-air balloon and floated on summer air across campus.

On the occasion of his appointment at the Illinois attorney general's Gang Crime Prevention Center, Burpee was decked out in a blue suit, a blue silk shirt buttoned to the collar, silky blue socks, and, rounding out the outfit, blue alligator shoes. Fantastic. I told him that I'd never seen a blue alligator; he sneered at me. Downtown, in an office near the Sears Tower, I introduced Burpee to the center's director and the director of research and their research staff.

Burpee poured on his charm to woo and win over his audience. The center's senior staff offered Burpee a job as a gang outreach worker in Champaign. I learned later that the prospect of having a six-time ex-convict, a chronic recidivist, on the payroll of the state's senior-most law enforcement official didn't appeal to his politically sensitive upper level staff. Taxpayers, we were told, wouldn't approve of an ex-con, a gangster on the dole. Good thing, too. Burpee gladly would have taken the paychecks, but working on his own recognizance, he would have yielded few products useful to the Gang Crime Prevention Center. Office work, agendas, self-motivated data collection, report writing, and deadlines weren't his forte or fate. When my mission to elevate Burpee, bump him up into the middle class, failed, frankly, I was relieved. I'd have been on the hook for the work he didn't do. What was I thinking?

In my professional world of the university, faculty publications and titles inflate egos. On the streets it seems that guys like Burpee had different measures of what constitutes achievement and success. Five years after his release, he hadn't committed a felony, and he took pride in that accomplishment. No one in his family had stayed straight or out of prison that long. He was the first in his family to go straight; it took a while, but he did it. The north end didn't hold a graduation ceremony for him or Alabama. Jaboo stayed out longer the fifth time than his previous times. That was an accomplishment, too. There were no certificates acknowledging the successful pursuit of a straight life. No diploma authenticated Burpee's accomplishments—only a release day lunch at Burger King. That was sufficient.

8

They Don't Need
a Savior

Researchers like me cannot seem to stay away from the helpless and hopeless lost souls on the streets. Merely the attraction of studying the helpless and hopeless means that well before I begin doing the tasks required by ethnography I am already hooked and will inevitably do my best to come to their aid. I will be their champion and savior, and no matter how hard I try to prevent it, my ethnographic adventures into the lives of others will become intensely personal.

It's hard for an ethnographer to avoid personal involvement in people's lives. We see people every day. We talk to them and they talk to us. Any type of research that uses human language, whether spoken or written, as the medium by which to elicit data will end up conveying informants' subjective opinions, beliefs, attitudes, perceptions, interpretations, and judgments. Face-to-face interviews conducted informally on street corners or when hanging around public housing estates and more structured formal interviews conducted in juvenile probation offices both gather subjective data. Personal interviews generate short narratives, sometimes only consisting of a few words, sometimes consisting of longer utterances, snippets of the stories people tell about their lives.[1] Structured interviews like those I did on the north end produce similar snippets too, although the form—checking boxes and fill-ins on blank lines—differ from informal or semiformal interviews. Personal interviews can yield a high rate of investment, yet the only thing we know about our responding informants is what we hear them say.

Ethnography looks back into the history of the contexts of people's lives in order to understand the historical pressures that shape those contexts. The history of the north end helped to shape the structure and content of this book. With the past in mind, I jumped into the present day. Ethnographers get knee-deep in people's lives over months and years, watching and listening, in the hope that we can gain an understanding of what people do and say in specific contexts. If we hang around long enough, we learn that things people say about what they do often has little to do with what they in fact did. So then we turn to folklore, the things people say, as a means to examine the source of what people say.

Ethnography cannot be validly critiqued for being intensely personal. Ethnography is supposed to be personal, and the process that makes it personal and subjective is transference: we see in others things about ourselves we like and don't like, and in that process judgmental interpretations creep into our understanding of the way others live.[2] Transference is an ethnographer's unconscious process of psychological identification with the proverbial "other," the people we spend our lives studying.[3] Transference animates the world around us and influences a researcher's perception of informants' behavior and affects his or her perception of a community.[4]

In my early days on the north end I saw shabby houses, broken sidewalks, dirt where grass was supposed to be, kids in old clothes, people hanging around on work days, illegal drugs being sold and smoked within yards of where youngsters bought ice cream and rode bikes. I don't see such things in my neighborhood. Nevertheless, after a few weeks there, houses didn't look so shabby. Kids looked like any kids in play clothes. Repairing old cars begins to look like a smarter choice than spending tens of thousands of dollars on a newer car that will require the same repairs when it gets old. Vice Lords hanging out on the stoop are just teenagers laughing and smoking weed.

My interpretation of north end culture was shaped by transference. The community I saw was energetic and had a personality that valued personal freedom, encouraged personal responsibility, and strongly endorsed nonjudgmental interpersonal relations. The north end was a poor black community where illegal drugs were sold to get money to buy food and diapers and to pay bills and where teenage girls dropped out of high school and became unemployed teenage mothers. The bigger truth is that poor blacks live that way largely as the result of historical forces like slavery, racism, and American culture's history of xenophobic responses to the other, which created a socioeconomic structure that benefits some at the expense of others. A xenophobic interpretation of poor black culture represents it as a dysfunctional tangle of pathologies.[5]

As outsiders saw it, the north end community appeared a threatening and potentially violent place; even my new graduate research assistants felt that way. Time passed, and familiarity with the locals altered my graduate assistants' subjective interpretation of the place and its people. In my personal experience, it didn't take too long before the north end and its people like Burpee, Jaboo, and Alabama became as familiar to me as my university colleagues, and most often a lot friendlier and less judgmental. I saw life on the north end as a simpler way of life. My way of life wasn't better or worse than theirs; it was just different from theirs.

When I attached bits and pieces of myself to the north end and its people, good and bad things happened. The good thing was a closer look at the way people live that, I hoped, was free of my personal biases and unconsciously transferred judgment. The bad thing was my over-whelming need to save the helpless and the hopeless. I felt that I had the power to save people and improve their quality of life. At that point my sin was vanity. We, the well educated, the well paid, feel empowered and entitled to meddle in others' lives. Others didn't ask me to help save them by finding them employment, pulling them from the quagmire of privation. I did it anyway. It was a selfish act. Governments do it too, by mandating social interventions, like the welfare-to-work demonstration project, on people who didn't ask for help.[6] I tell myself that the story I have told in *Living Black* will be the final tale of how I meddled in the others' lives.

The Washington and Burpee families were gracious, welcoming, and kind to a middle-aged white man who wanted to document their lives. I did more than that and shouldn't have. I disapproved of Iresha's first boyfriend, the weasel. Mo and Memphis saw him as teenage boy hanging out with their daughter. Burpee didn't ask me to inquire on his behalf about a job at the Gang Crime Prevention Center. Next time, I'll wait until the helpless and the hopeless ask me to save them.

Transference alters our interpretation of illegal behavior. After years on the street I eventually thought that laws criminalizing the sale of weed were utterly ridiculous. These were laws that adversely influenced people's way of life, which lawmakers, not having done years of field-work, know absolutely nothing about. I met a boy who earned enough income in five days working at a fast food joint to fund his weed business on weekends. He told me a quarter pound of weed cost him $250. He cleaned the weed and sold it by dime and dub bags; over a weekend, he recouped his initial cost, and he earned a profit of $250. In two days, he earned as much as he did working forty hours a week. On Friday, that kid asked me for a loan. If I gave him $250, he said, he'd add it to his $250 and buy more weed at a lower price and his profit would soar. He promised that I'd get back my $250 plus another $250 profit by Monday. Instead, I suggested a college education.

You could do better than sell weed, I told him in the tone of a caring father. When he finished high school, I told him, I would support his application to college. In the long run, I knew, he'd fare better and wouldn't do time. Even as I spoke those words, I regretted my sugges-tion. That kid was hungry today and wanted to eat today. College seems a great idea for youngsters like those on the north end only if someone will feed and clothe them over four years of college and then make sure that all the racial barriers have been cleared out of their path to middle-class income. The weed-dealing kid saw no economic value in college and had no inkling of what college entailed. To attend college, he'd have to leave his home, family, and friends and wander into a world as strange to him as the north end appeared to college professors who buzzed up their car windows and locked doors as they drove five minutes through it in the daylight of the afternoon.

The north end wasn't the first place I had played uninvited social worker. Forty years before in the Central Valley of Mexico I lived in a tiny settlement of cactus huts, like the settlements studied by Oscar Lewis, small rural villages where people ate what they grew and bought what they didn't grow. Lewis learned that if a pint of milk costs a peso, and people have a peso, they buy a pint. If they have two pesos they buy a quart. In my tiny settlement, people had eight pesos a week to spend at the market, enough for one kilo of beef and one kilo of pork. If they'd had more money, they'd have bought more. That's the argument Lewis proposed as the culture of poverty: you learn to live within your financial means, however limiting, extractive, and oppressive it might be, because there are no alternatives.

I took an eight-year-old boy to a Franciscan medical clinic on the north end of my village, Orizabita, a tiny spot twelve kilometers from Izmiquilpan, a wide spot on the Pan-American Highway. Pancho's oozing sores on his ear lobes were caused by malnutrition. Pus-filled sores attracted tiny flying bugs. It took me days to convince him to go see the nurses at the Franciscan clinic, which looked like any high-quality medical clinic in the States.

Pancho sat in a plastic chair, fidgeted, and looked terrified, tears rolling down his chubby cheeks. I held his hand as we walked into an examination room. He grimaced as the sister cleaned his sores. Outside, bandaged, he ran away from me, crying and yelling that the medication burned him and that he didn't want to see nurses. I hurt him, he said. He refused to speak to me again. I knew so little about the local culture that I made the mistake of thinking that a medicinal cure in a medical clinic was far superior to the local curer's.

I meddled decades later in Kansas City. Cara refused to live the way I thought she should live.[7] I made that error again with Burpee. He didn't have sores like Pancho or need school clothes like Cara. He needed a better job, I thought; he needed recognition of his good deeds. My dream for him was a nine-to-five job. Looking back, a nine-to-five job sounds like a bad dream.

Epilogue

During fieldwork in the Central Valley of Mexico in the 1970s, I learned that the departure of an ethnographer out of a field site leaves a lasting impression. If a departure goes well, it can smooth over clumsy missteps and faux pas along the way. North end families welcomed me and fed me and let me hang out and watch television when I needed friendly company and didn't want to stay in an empty house in Normal. I visited the Washington and Burpee families or stopped by Nike's to watch television and read books to Charles Jr., or hung around near Patti's, walking the street looking for fun banter, or waited for a drug spot to open and crowds to appear.

Relationships matured over many years. In one way of thinking, relationships are durable, even though when it came time to leave, I felt like a here today, gone tomorrow field researcher. When I told Mo I was leaving Illinois, she said Memphis would build a wall around a corner of the coffin alcove, where I could put in a bed and stay with them. With a big smile on her face, she added that with a white man in the house, cops would leave them alone and they could sell more weed. In another way of thinking, I felt that I could repay my accrued debt by offering a hand to folks like Burpee. He didn't need me, though. I was wrong. He saved himself from a life in prison and was doing quite well, without my help.

A few years after I completed my research and moved away, I returned to Champaign to visit my son, a graduate student at the university. I tried and failed to resist the urge to see the north end and walk its streets again. I felt at home there. I was so disappointed when I arrived. The streets that once had a life force, an identity, a personality, now were just streets in need of repair. Spots that had been alive with drug selling and hustling and hanging teenagers telling fanciful tales were now vacant street corners. Drug spots were boarded. The Pines had succumbed to the wrecking ball of progress. The apartments where I spent years getting to know families had been torn down and replaced by a modern public housing estate. With that transformation Big C's spirit lost its home.

I had to find Burpee. When I moved away I thought of him as a friend. I had been away for so long and now needed to know if he had thought of me as a friend or just an annoying white man. I parked in front of his house. In my mind's eye Crystal was playing on the driveway. I knocked on the front door. No one answered. I knocked again, careful to use a friendly knock. A head poked around the corner of the wall separating the living room from a hall leading to the front door. It was a boy, maybe ten. He stared. I signaled to him with a come here wave of my hand, palm up, fingers moving front to back, back to front. He disappeared. Soon Burpee's wife appeared. She opened the door a crack, as folks are prone to do. She was silent.

"Is Burpee here?" Silence. "You remember me. Mark. I hung out with Burpee years ago." Silence. "Is he here?"

"No."

"Do you know his cell number?"

"No."

"Does he live here or across the street?"

"He moved."

"I'd like to talk to him."

"He moved."

"Where'd he go?"

"I'm not sure."

"Chicago?"

"Springfield," she said, like she was giving away state secrets.

"You know his address?"

"No."

"Does he have a new cell number? The number I have is dead."

"I don't know."

"Thanks. If you hear from him, tell him Mark, the white man, was looking for him."

Nod.

The door closed. Disappointed, again.

I continued my search for affirmation as I drove to the White House. I needed to know if I had been a good guy over the years I had spent there, more than just a white man who doled out dubs.

The White House hadn't changed. I knocked on the door, using a friendly knock. A middle-age guy opened the door and saw me standing there. "Oops, sorry, wrong house," I said, immediately apologetic. My manic search for affirmation pushed on. I had to find the Washington family's current house. It wasn't easy. I asked people whose faces I remembered, people who once knew me, a simple question: "You know the Washingtons? Where the Washingtons staying at?" Silence, a shrug, a quizzical look.

I cruised up one street and down another, and then, finally, I spotted Memphis's pick-up truck parked at the curb on the side of another white house. I banged on the back door. I saw that it opened onto a mud porch. No one answered the knock. Some things don't change. I walked into this house like I had walked into their apartment at the Pine's and the Blue House and the White House so many times over so many years. In the kitchen, Mo, Memphis, Iresha, LaWanda, Mario Jr., Calvin, and Bennie and Willie were huddled around LaWanda's new baby reclining in his booster chair atop the kitchen table. Mario Jr. had grown into the little kid stage. Calvin towered over Iresha. Bennie and Willie smiled those same little boy smiles I had been fond of seeing.

Without a "Hello, how you been? Where you living?," LaWanda blurted out, "Mark, you let me hold five hundred?" Some things don't change.

I had felt uncomfortable leaving the north end in 2002. I felt attached. The place and people had personal meaning. Years later, those attachments had dissolved. Comfort and security that comes with personal relationships had abated. I couldn't imagine how disoriented and confused men like Alabama and Jaboo felt when they came back to town after ten to twenty years behind razor wire. They were fortunate. Burpee had helped them to learn the rules of civil society and acquire the legit skills to sustain themselves in the absence of prison handouts, food, shelter, and a built-in social life.

A global lesson of anthropology is that people have learned to live everywhere. The cliché that you can't go home again doesn't apply to Jaboo, Cliff, and Tracy. When they get tired of fighting the streets, become weary of people who are afraid to look them in the eye, worn out from trying to find a job, and when their fingers grow tired of checking the box, "Yes, I committed a felony," they can return to prison, a familiar place where neighborhood friends and family await their arrival.

Life inside prison walls offers a way of living preferable to sleeping, like Cliff did, behind a dumpster on cold nights in central Illinois. Cliff and Tracy, and thousands like them, are forced to sleep in trashy garages and stay high to allay hunger pains, and they can readily avail themselves of the predictable securities of prison life. Men and women like the people I write about in *Living Black* were on the streets as a result of circumstances generated by insufficiencies in property, fundamental possessions such as civil rights, healthcare, and education. These insufficiencies of property sprang from the historical and modern forces of politically motivated, deliberate indifference to the quality of life of black citizens.[1]

If I were compelled to explain how Burpee, a man who was born into poverty in a highly segregated urban setting and who spent well over half his life in prison, one day stopped doing the things he knew well and enjoyed, like gangbanging and selling drugs and street insurance, I'd say it was his innate stubbornness, his memories of the infliction of scars, his baby daughter Crystal, and his personal relationships on the north end with local citizens and ex-convicts who needed and respected him. He was stubborn. He got what he wanted. He did not forgive or forget until he got his pound of flesh. Injection site scars, bullet wound and knife blade scars told of a style of life of a hard man, a criminal, a prisoner, and a victim of the racism and hatred toward blacks in Chicago that compelled families like his to do whatever they had to do get enough money to eat.[2]

I'm not his apologist. I cannot imagine the fear and anxiety of families like his who faced a white society in the 1940s and 1950s that hated blacks. I only guessed that society's hatred of people like him, the black and poor and uneducated, engendered his willingness to fight back. Burpee fought back the wrong way; he hurt himself and others. For that, there's no forgiveness. If society wants to prevent guys like him from taking a pound of flesh, we need to look past what he did and ask why he did it and how we, the white power structure of America, contributed to his self-destruction. Prisons won't go away by teaching men like Alabama how to read or getting them trivial jobs. Only when we come to understand our role in promulgating the sociopolitical forces that built an endless number of prisons can we start to see beyond our own worldview.

The north end has no history of fighting back against the local white citizenry, and over many decades a white and black symbiotic, socio-economic relationship emerged.[3] Whites have lived among blacks on the north end for nearly a century and still do. Although local police in the past had allegedly labeled the black north end the "Jungle," I didn't witness police hostility toward blacks nor black hostility toward the police during my time there.[4] In fact, I documented a remarkable policing strategy that warned drug sellers of impending arrests (though the drug sellers didn't have the common sense to pay attention and heed the warning).

I saw no evidence that north end privation caused moral degeneration, eroded personal ethics, or annulled the Protestant work ethic. White complaints about poor family care and irresponsible fathers fly far afield from my years of participating in and watching social life on the north end. As a white man in an African American neighborhood, I saw social problems I've seen in white communities, as well. On the interstate highway leading to Chicago's O'Hare airport I have seen signs pasted on the coin drop baskets at toll booths that read "Don't Forget to Pay Your Child Support."

North end black families acquired the cultural skills to live as well as they could with fewer goods and services than the middle class has become accustomed to. Without a public, private, or socioeconomic safety net, a safety net that does not merely amount to government handouts, a single bad decision can send a teenager like Iresha off in an unplanned and uncontrollable direction. Iresha made one bad decision that changed her and the direction of her life. Her dreams faded in a haze of uncontrollable consequences (although even if the weasel hadn't chosen her as his next sexual victim, Iresha still may not have finished high school or earned a GED or applied to the University of Michigan).

Local culture was hard. Everyone had few choices. Each choice had serious consequences. Have sex and get pregnant, then you're on your own. Quit school, then you have to hustle. Stay in school, then you struggle to find a job. Sell drugs, then you end up doing time and you'll likely do time again. No one comes to the rescue. No one I knew had an ATM card. No one I knew chose to live with less.

Interventionists take heed. Caution is required in dealing with other lives. I spent years hanging around with people I walked away from. I retreated to my comfortable home and cushy university job. I did research that benefited my career. I offered the folks I studied a $20 payment per interview. We laughed and had fun. Once free of self-delusion that I could do more than offer a dub, my dreams for them faded into their reality of privation. I learned again on the north end that a career criminal's life could not be improved through my assistance, that a man like Burpee cannot become more than a hustler. I hustled him. He hustled me. Burpee and I had fun while it lasted. In the end, I have gained far more from him than he gained from me. And that's always true when anthropologists intrude in places where they weren't invited.

Notes

Prologue

1. Champaign and Urbana, Illinois, were referred to as the Twin Cities in historical case studies of north end black community (Bindman 1961; Cromwell 1934). In Cromwell's 1934 thesis the north end was referred to as the "north end of town," which extended across the northern end of Champaign and Urbana. My study focuses on Champaign's north end, which should not to be confused with Whyte's Irish North End in Boston, Massachusetts.

2. I was a local evaluator on a national youth gang prevention, intervention, and suppression project and worked with Professor Irving Spergel, School of Social Service Administration, University of Chicago. My role in Spergel's project was funded by a subcontract from the University of Chicago to Illinois State University, where I was a professor of criminal justice sciences while I was working on the Spergel project as well as two other research studies, one that was conducted at the behest of the U.S. Census Bureau and that examined adult gang member residential mobility and another that was funded by the Office of Juvenile Justice and Delinquency Prevention (OJJDP) and that explored the personal social networks of adolescent and young adult women who identified themselves as gang members.

Chapter 1. The Ethnographer and the Ex-Convict

1. The difference between a qualitative study and an ethnographic study is the difference between learning French in a language lab and learning French

135

while living in Paris. Howard Becker and Blanche Geer offer a succinct summary of the ethnographic method and its unique and substantive outcomes. "The most complete form of the sociological datum . . . is the form in which the participant observer gathers it: An observation of some social event, the events which precede and follow it, and explanations of its meaning by participants and spectators, before, during, and after its occurrence. Such a datum gives us more information about the event under study than data gathered by any other sociological method. Participant observation can thus provide us with a yard-stick against which to measure the completeness of data gathered in other ways, a model which can serve to let us know what orders of information escape us when we use other methods. By participant observation we mean that method in which the observer participates in the daily life of the people under study, either openly in the role of researcher or covertly in some disguised role, observing things that happen, listening to what is said and questioning people, over some length of time" (1957: 28). Participant observation and its comple-mentary methods enable an ethnographer to get a close view of daily life, which over long periods can lead to nuanced interpretations of culture's influence on behavior and thought (Geertz 1957, 1973). Culture influences thought, giving way to the concept of worldview. Malinowski (1922: 517) defines worldview as an "outlook on things, [man's] Weltanshauung. . . . Every human culture gives its members a definite vision of the world." Doing interviews off campus on street corners or in social service offices or in visiting rooms of jails and prisons is closer to qualitative research than ethnography. A true ethnographic inquiry lets us understand the cultural logic that integrates what people say about what they do and what they actually do and gives us a means to interpret behavior within the framework of the culture shared by the people we study.

2. Burpee referred to himself as an "ex-convict." In the culture of prison, the terms "convict" and "inmate" are status markers. In the vernacular of prison, the term "convict" denotes a prisoner who is tough, strong, and able to "handle his business"; the term "inmate" refers to a prisoner who is weak physically or mentally, a person unable to withstand the pressures of prison. On the streets of the north end, folks didn't use the terms of reference "ex-convict," "former inmate," or "formerly incarcerated persons." See Fleisher (1995) and Irwin (1970) for accounts of the meanings of the terms "convict" and "inmate" within the vernacular of prison culture.

3. See Allison (1924).

4. Stack (1974: xii) reports that she was given the nickname "white Caroline."

5. See "OJJDP Honors Irving Spergel, Creator of the OJJDP Comprehen-sive Gang Model," December 30, 2010, www.ojjdp.gov. I take this opportunity

to memorialize Irving Spergel's contributions to gang research and applied social science and express my gratitude that he allowed me to participate in his research on gang prevention, intervention, and suppression. Spergel was a social worker by trade, a scholar by profession, and a humanitarian by heart whose lifelong scholarship has contributed enormously to the understanding of American youth gang culture as well as gang intervention and prevention programs. It was a courageous decision on the part of the Office of Juvenile Justice and Delinquency Prevention to fund the Spergel project. Spergel was not an apologist for gang violence. He championed equitable treatment of children and adolescents and encouraged community involvement in children's lives, which maximized social services delivered to traumatized children and adolescents. The Spergel project was a method of approaching youth-oriented behavior change by unifying the complementary resources of communities and aiming those resources at the specific underlying social and economic risk factors that contributed to delinquency and gang behavior. The Spergel project brought to the attention of communities the need to support youth who most likely would have been overlooked, forgotten, and left to flounder on the streets and in prisons.

6. See Institute for Intergovernmental Research (2009).

7. See Fleisher (1998).

8. Lewis's concept of the culture of poverty is highly controversial and frequently misunderstood (see Harvey and Reed 1996). In "The Culture of Poverty" (1998), he describes those misunderstanding and emphasizes the point that a culture of poverty must be distinguished from impoverishment. Not all poor cultures are cultures of poverty. Lewis outlines fifty traits derived from his research in Mexico that are distinctive of a culture of poverty and notes specifically that "people in the culture of poverty have a strong feeling of marginality, of helplessness, of dependency, of not belonging" (1961: 7). I argue in this book and others (1995, 1998) that street culture shares traits with a culture of poverty. Irrespective of race and ethnicity, men and women enmeshed in street culture, like those in a culture of poverty, are convinced they are alone, the sole victims of contemporary problems, and they feel as if they have no legitimate role in mainstream society. Lewis also undertook anthropological studies of individuals and families and argued that psychological and ideological traits are significant in a culture of poverty (1950). The argument that a culture and its participants share personality traits and an ideology represents distinctive features of the concept of a culture of poverty. Friedenberg (1962) offers a clear, nontechnical interpretation of Lewis's culture of poverty.

9. See Fleisher (1995).

10. Research for Short and Strodtbeck (1965) included gang member interviews conducted by a detached social worker. These narrative data include stories about a violent gang leader who called himself Burpee and who called his gang the Burpees. The Burpees hung around neighborhoods where Burpee told me he hung out, including the Jewish ghetto. Burpee and I visited that area; he called it "Jew Town."

11. Mother's Day refers to the days when folks receive government payments, which some folks use to buy illegal drugs.

12. See Fleisher (2001a, 2001b). The Spergel project required a quota of structured interviews. Ethnographic interviews have no quota. Ethnographic interviews include a stream of continuous conversations that deliver narrative data in quick chats on the street and while watching television and in conversations in cars and with cops at the police station and on the street, among other places. Ethnographic interviews gather all the data structured interviews can and deliver contextual data as well.

13. See Fleisher (1989).

14. Institutional review boards invariably are opposed to the idea of offering cash payments to poor black youth in exchange for interviews with them. I've heard members of research review boards assert, in regard to my street and gang research, that a teenager or an adult paid to do an interview would likely use a cash payment to buy illegal drugs. I think that's a rude and an outlandish comment, particularly to make to me, given that I have studied poor black teenagers and adults most of my career. Review boards have suggested that instead of cash payments I offer prepaid cards to movie theaters or fast-food joints, unaware of the fact that youth in communities like the north end or Kansas City (Fleisher 1998) or Seattle (1995) don't attend movies and that they only enjoy fast food when someone drives and buys it for them. Poor north end people I knew didn't have sufficient surplus cash to waste on fast food or cars to roll up to drive-through windows; they often felt uncomfortable mingling among folks outside the north end. I prefer to offer poor people cash payments. Universities have never paid me with prepaid food and movie cards. I extended that same courtesy to citizens on the north end.

15. See Fleisher (1998).

16. When Iresha's best friend Cookie was arrested and jailed, she asked if I'd post Cookie's bond. I refused. She then asked if I'd put money on Cookie's "books," a commissary account in a jail or prison that holds money inmates use to purchase hygiene products and munchies. I did that. Cookie sent several letters thanking me. The letters suggested that when she was released, she would repay me with personal favors. I showed Iresha the letters. She laughed,

saying her friend was hustling me, in the hope that I would continue to deposit cash in the account.

17. When the Spergel project ended, I received a grant (OJJDP Grant 2000-JR-VX-0006) to carry out a field research study on women and gangs. This study was designed to empirically measure the composition and structural characteristics of adolescent and young adult women's social, instrumental, and affective support networks, which had previously been studied with qualitative methods (Angel and Tienda 1982; Chatters, Taylor, and Neighbors 1989; Hill 1997; Fleisher 1998; Stack 1974; Taylor 1990). Personal network analysis of the friendship networks of late adolescent and young adult women who claimed a gang affiliation added empirical measures that complemented previous ethnographic gang girl research (Fleisher 1998) and then led to mixed-methods analysis (Espelage, Wasserman, and Fleisher 2007; Fleisher and Papachristos 2010). The theory and methods described by Wasserman and Faust (1994) were the basis of the qualitative tools I designed for the north end network study. These tools generated types of data necessary for statistical analysis of friendship networks (Fleisher 2002). *Living Black* offers in a narrative ethnographic format elements of the social complexity described by network statistics. OJJDP funds were not utilized to support or conduct the ethnography reported in this book.

Chapter 2. Culture and Social Life

1. Frazier (1937: 612–13) argues that the blues, for instance, gave voice to normative patterns of sex and family behavior, the disappointment and disillusionment that comes with going beyond normative folk culture, and warnings about straying beyond the limits of the black community and social security of kinfolk. These black folktales are akin to white culture's Goldilocks and three bears (Dundes 1965).

2. In the history of anthropological studies on non-Western society, the concept of folk has been used to refer to communities that embrace customary folkways and mores typical of village life and whose members' social interactions are based on kinship, friendship, and neighborliness and who share an implicit worldview (Foster 1953). The characteristic ways the members of a society look at themselves and the world and society are unconscious to them and discernible to ethnographers through a careful analysis of kinship, child rearing, marriage, and speech and behavior (Dundes 1969). An anthropological approach to folklore derives from anthropology's history of studying non-Western, nonliterate cultures where cultural knowledge was passed on verbally in daily

conversations, mythologies, rituals, and ceremonies. Dundes observes that "'folk ideas' . . . mean traditional notions that a group of people have about the nature of man, of the world, and of man's life in the world. Folk ideas [are] expressed in . . . proverbs, . . . folktales, folksongs, . . . which underlie the thought and action of a given group of people. . . . All cultures have underlying assumptions and it is these assumptions or folk ideas which are the building blocks of worldview" (1971: 95–96). Folklore examines beliefs or belief systems and the ways people search for explanations to worldly or supernatural answers in cultures whose worldview does not rely on principles of modern science. While doing fieldwork on a Salish Indian reservation on the Olympic Peninsula in Washington, I participated in a ritual to rid the reservation of evil forces that had caused domestic violence, delinquency, and alcohol abuse. The Salish worldview conceptualized the cause of social dysfunction as supernatural and so the remedy aimed at supernatural causes and offered a supernatural remedy. Those were folkloric beliefs. My role as a cultural anthropologist required documenting Salish beliefs and did not require arguing that violence and addiction had other causes. Cultural analysis seeks to understand belief systems within a specific cultural context and explain how beliefs are integral to a society's worldview. Cultural anthropologists gather folkloric tales and out of these try to discern a people's worldview (Dundes 1971).

3. What's important is the consistency of stories with extant cultural narratives (Benford 2002; Benford and Snow 2008). Stories' empirical credibility depends on fidelity, the way stories are told and the extent to which they are similar to other stories deemed credible (White 1980). Stories like legends and rumors are not expected to be accurate depictions of real-world events; rather listeners ask if these stories are credible and reasonable in the world they're in (Fine and Khawaja 2005). Fleisher and Krienert (2009) offers a folkloric analysis of the stories male and female prison inmates tell about sexual violence in prison.

4. See Atkinson, Delamont, and Housley (2008: 91).

5. "Culture-bound" refers to behavioral or psychological conditions or medical practices unique to specific cultures. Culture-bound explanations stand in contrast to ethnocentric interpretations, which judge the behavior, beliefs, attitudes, and values in one culture by standards used in a different culture. Culture-bound interpretations give way to political implications that, for example, have influenced educators' opinions on the ability of black youth to achieve in classroom education because these youth speak vernacular black English (Labov 1972). Culture-bound misinterpretations of the culture of poverty posits that black culture is impoverished, a depredated culture stripped

of an inability to dig its way out of poverty (see Lewis [1998] for a critique of
the use of the culture of poverty to define the nature of poor black culture and
Stack [1974], who argues that conditions such as unemployment, low wages,
and crowded living quarters are not characteristics of a black culture). William
Julius Wilson's (1987) social isolation model, for example, is grounded in synchronic perspective that tries to account for visible features of the black community like crime by finding other visible features like unemployment that
cause crime and to seek solutions for crime and unemployment within that
framework. Diachronic analysis, by contrast, argues that today's black culture
has roots in its historical antecedents (see Mayhew 1983). Frazier's analyses of
black family types are grounded in the history of black families during slavery.
Conservative components of culture like kinship and friendship patterns, religion, values and beliefs about community life have remained in place 150 years
after the Civil War. Synchronic adaptations to urban life that depend on literacy
and education fail because of a lack of education and modes of employment
skill, which have been slow to change in black communities given the legal and
political obstacles thrown in the path of modern black communities. As Frazier
notes, "In the rigorous competitive life of northern cities, the poor and illiterate
Negroes with no other resources but their folk culture are ground down by
disease, vice, and poverty" (1937: 617). The theory that generates the framework
of the ethnographic narrative in *Living Black* posits a continuation of cultural
patterns Frazier identifies and, as Lewis (1950) argues, a continuation of historically grounded cultural adaptations of community life that stress the role of
kinship and friendship in sustaining an organized, well-integrated social life on
the north end.

   6. See Cromwell (1934), Kusmer (1978), and Marks (1989).

   7. Price-Spratlen (1998) argues for a process he terms ethnogenesis, which
posits that black migration north gradually created social and communication
networks that shaped northern black communities. Further, and more important
in this book, he argues that migrant ethnic groups reconstituted their cultural
communities in a different location, transferring the social structure and organization and communal ethos of their birthplace to a new location. Once
transplanted, these black communities attracted more black migrants. Price-
Spratlen's argument has historical scholarly precedent. In 1952 Oscar Lewis
published an article in which he argued against the contention that rural-to-
urban migration led to community disorganization, personal maladjustment,
fragmentation of family life, an increase in delinquency, and a general decline
in migrants' internal cultural systems, like religion and kinship. He claimed
that sociological generalizations on crime, education, family, mortality and

morbidity were based on comparative statistical data that was ethnocentric. In a 1934 thesis, Janet Cromwell noted family stability and solidarity in the north end, along with economic stability and house purchases, strong religious verve, an integration of whites into the black community, and the preservation of kinship and friendship systems that had been transplanted from the south into a northern setting. Along with the regeneration of those cultural systems came a renewal of the culture's worldview. Frazier's 1937 analysis of black families similarly argued that cultural systems like kinship and family are transplanted in situ after migration. Bindman (1961: 16) has a map of my study area as it appeared 1961.

8. Bindman's (1961) and Cromwell's (1934) on-site, firsthand research documents white residents in that area and amicable relationships among blacks and whites in the Champaign-Urbana community. Cromwell observes that 42 percent of blacks she interviewed owned houses (62). A white real-estate agent owned thirty to fifty houses; fifty-eight of one hundred people sampled bought or were in the process of buying those houses. The average house price was $3,260, or $43,352.25 in 2002 dollars.

9. Cultural anthropologist Walter Miller's (1958, 1962) analysis of what he terms lower-class culture among adolescents in white and Negro slums in Boston echoes Thrasher's (1913) observations on adolescent gangs in Chicago in the early twentieth century, aimlessly hanging around street corners and exhibiting aggression, violence, and substance abuse, characteristics he attributed to neighborhood and individual distress. Miller's analysis of adolescent deviance is predicated on and illustrates the application of a newly emerging cultural theory of normative cultural relativism. The theory of normative cultural relativism postulates that culture strongly influences human behavior and disavows the use of a single set of standards to judge and interpret human behavior. Disavowing the use of a single set of standards necessitates understanding human behavior within unique cultural contexts (Spiro 1986).

10. Arewea and Dundes (2011) refer to this type of folklore as proverbs, impersonal vehicles that direct people's action or thought by way of an anonymous story; these are related as "they said" and "he said" stories.

11. Cromwell (1934: 37).

12. See Bindman (1961) and Cromwell (1934).

13. This area was called the north end in the 1990s. In earlier times, it had been referred to as the Champaign-Urbana Negro community, the Negro ghetto, and Negro section (Bindman 1961). Early twentieth century Chicago sociologists (Hughes 1954; Lind 1930; Park 1915; Wirth 1928) characterized ghettos and slums in derogatory racial terms; ghettos were home to European

migrants, places where these migrants reconstructed their native homes; slums were residential areas of black migrants and "retarded" Negro offenders (Jackson 1923). Characterizations like these might well have become part of a north end folklore that depicted the area as an unhospitable place.

14. *Living Black* documents life on the east and west side of the tracks, in census tracts 2 (east) and 7 (west). White real estate developers built houses specifically for black occupants; blacks rented from white landlords. After the Great Depression, according to Cromwell (1934), whites occupied the houses they built for blacks, and more whites moved into the north end because rents were lower. By 1970, however, tract 2 was nearly 95 percent black; while tract 7 was 16 percent black; in 1990, tract 7 was 44 percent black (Fleisher 2002).

15. Frazier (1937) refers to these normative patterns as folkways, folk culture, and the role of kinfolk in black folk culture.

16. Cromwell's (1934: 14, table 4) data indicate that the greatest number of blacks residing in Illinois in 1910 had migrated from Tennessee and Kentucky and that by 1930 the greatest number had migrated from Mississippi, Alabama, and Georgia. See Stewart (1967).

17. Cromwell (1934).

18. See Zorbaugh (1983 [1929]).

19. See Allison (1924).

20. See Benford (2002) and White (1980, 2009).

21. Fleisher (2002) finds that 94 percent of study participants had not gone outside the north end for any reason in the six months prior to the interviews. People spent time with nearby friends, listened to music, did laundry, and watched television together; rarely did these young women read by themselves, talk about local and national politics, or participate in community activities outside the north end. Cromwell's (1934) findings are similar among men and women whose social activities didn't require money. In an ironic twist, the aim of the research I did on adult gang member residential mobility was to contribute to reducing the undercounting of black residents and improve methods of contacting black residents at voting time.

22. Bindman's data (1961) show that blacks were fully engaged in local politics and the expansion of economic opportunities for blacks in the 1960s.

23. Fleisher's (2002) social network sample included 44 percent with full-time jobs with an average self-reported $250 median weekly income, which was equivalent to $18.79 per week, or the approximate median income among black residents on the north end in 1935. Cromwell's sample of employed black workers finds a majority of unskilled workers earned between $10 and $25 per week, or $133 to $332 per week in 2002 dollars. Cromwell doesn't report the number of

hours worked to earn $10 to $25 per week. Fleisher's sample has the highest median hourly income at $8, or sixty cents per hour in 1935 dollars.

24. In a cross-cultural example, in Straits Salish (see Fleisher 1976), a language spoken on the Olympic Peninsula of Washington state and regions of British Columbia, the English term "orphan" is the literal translation of the Straits Salish term that means "no wealth, no family."

25. Cromwell (1934) reports a high value on these social attachments.

26. See ibid.

27. "Champaign-Urbana has no defined Negro business area, with the possible exception of several grocery stories and barber shops. . . . Most of the grocery stores are owned by white people" (Cromwell 1934: 32). Cromwell notes that black-owned businesses would have been difficult to support, because blacks had little money and whites would not shop at black-owned stores like groceries. There were local, black-owned barber shops and a few barbecue spots.

Chapter 3. Lively Streets

1. See Cromwell (1934: 29).

2. Cromwell (1934) reports one black "policeman" on the Champaign police department in the mid-1930s. I didn't ask the Champaign Police Department for staff demographic data; such a request was beyond the scope of what Spergel required.

3. I wasn't in a political position at the outset of the project to ask police how they counted gang members and if the department's database distinguished between gang and nongang crime.

4. Masotti and Corsi (1969) report black snipers targeted police in Cleveland. Tales like that easily traveled from Cleveland to Champaign by the train that linked the two cities.

5. For my study of adult gang member residential mobility, if adult male gang members—nearly all of whom were ex-convicts—had female household partners, I interviewed them, too, and collected data on the details of their social and economic relationship, which explains how ex-cons exploit household resources of their baby mamas or alternatively how men fit into the household structure and organization of their natal and extended families.

6. Frazier (1937) offers a vivid portrayal of racial violence in Chicago and street crime in black neighborhoods. See also Cutler and Glaeser (1999) and Olzak, Shanahan, and McEneaney (1996). Champaign's proximity to Chicago opened the flow of people and presumably accounts of Chicago's racial violence.

Even in the 1960s when white-instigated violence plagued Chicago's black neighborhoods, Bindman (1961) does not report interracial violence in the Champaign-Urbana community. Black employment could have been a moderating factor. The University of Illinois at Urbana-Champaign had been an ongoing source of black employment in skilled and unskilled jobs since black migrants settled the north end (Cromwell 1934). In his accounts of the local socioeconomic climate, Bindman reports that blacks and whites worked out compromises that opened blacks' access to jobs in the growing business community, and that over the years of local economic expansion, black ministers became involved in brokering black employment in the white community through the Champaign-Urbana Negro North End Ministers Association.

7. See Masotti and Corsi (1969).

8. Black neighborhoods in Chicago that had stable families and home ownership had a 1.4 percent delinquency rate in the 1930s (Frazier 1937: 615). In Champaign's north end in the 1930s, people were able to purchase homes and find employment; there was economic security and religious stability. A deterioration of these conditions might have occurred, although Bindman doesn't mention any such deterioration. Bindman reports (1961: 2–4) a proportionally high number of blacks who were employed: 39 percent were employed in unskilled jobs (ten times more than what population proportionality would predict) and 21 percent were employed in semiskilled jobs (five times more than what population proportionality would predict); 6 percent were employed in professional positions.

9. See Spradley (1970).

10. See Fleisher (2002).

11. Prisoner reentry publications describe prisoner populations, threats that returning prisoners pose to communities, what qualifies as adequate and inadequate funding for parole supervision, employers' rejection of ex-convicts as potential employees, and recidivism (Fleisher and Krienert 2004; Travis and Lawrence 2002; Travis, Solomon, and Waul 2001; Lynch and Sabol 2001; Petersilia 2003; Pew Center on States 2011). Fleisher (1995, 2001b) and Irwin (1970) have described the tumultuous effects prison release has on ex-convicts at street level. Reentry as witnessed from street level doesn't begin in prerelease prison programs and postrelease visits at parole offices. In Cleveland it begins when a public bus company drops off a few men in front of a bus station, at one in the morning, when it's near freezing, and then pulls away leaving ex-cons alone on dark sidewalks dressed in prison clothing, a few dollars in their pocket, no one to pick them up, and nowhere to go. In Youngstown, Ohio, in 2007, police detectives had reports of break-ins at bars in rundown neighborhoods in

a particular area; investigations showed no money or property or liquor had been stolen. Local folks eventually told detectives that a recently released prisoner known to many of them was the culprit. Arrested, the ex-convict said that the weather was cold and he had nowhere to sleep, so he broke into bars after hours searching for an escape from the icy weather and a safe place to bed down (personal communication, Detective/Sergeant M. Lambert, December 6, 2007). A police chief (who prefers to remain anonymous) in a central Ohio community initiated a reentry court there. He documented the nature of the reentry problem in his town. Police officers filmed a bus that dropped two released inmates in the village square, still dressed in the prison's red coveralls; the men wandered about until they spotted a car driven by someone they knew. They hopped in, and the car drove off.

12. R. Root, business administrator, fiscal operations, Illinois Correctional Industries, Illinois Department of Correction, personal conversation, March 22, 2012.

13. See Fleisher (1989).

14. Sexual bullying was difficult to identify through observation and was rarely discussed by young women. Male-male, female-female, and male-female relations are aggressive (Stack 1975). A boundary between aggressive sexualized play, sexual bullying, sexual exploitation, and rape is difficult to gauge. Female interviewees did not report nonconsensual sex, either descriptively or by using the term "rape" (see Fleisher 2002 for empirical data on sexual behavior). An ethical issue added difficulty to the collection of data on sexual behavior. Even though I had been working on the north end for many years and knew dozens of late adolescent and mature women, I felt that asking them about their sexual behavior was too personal, too potentially damaging to me, as a researcher with strong personal ties in the community, and could be politically disastrous if it were reported in the pages of the newspaper. My research on social networks included a public health and sex survey, which was designed in collaboration with a University of Illinois faculty expert on adolescent public health and administered by a well-known female research assistant.

15. See Frazier (1937: 611-13).

16. See Fleisher (2001b).

17. See Jacobs (1978).

18. See Flannery and Kretschmar (2012).

Chapter 4. Everyday Life

1. North end families can be categorized using Frazier's "Negro" family typology. He argues that economic and cultural differences among premigration

families determined how well families adjusted in new environments. The first type of marriage pattern he called the "maternal family" pattern, the "purest and most primitive form in the rural South" (1937: 609). A maternal family refers to a family based primarily on mother-offspring emotional affection and common interests; she is head of the family. These families originate in illegitimate children, who are often the result of liaisons with several men whose interest in the family ends after impregnation. Occasionally men show interest in the family, but even if they do, as males, they have no authority within the family. "This type of family pattern has existed since . . . slavery when the mother was the dominant and most stable [family member]" (610). Frazier's second family type resembles the family pattern often found among American whites. These families, who likewise had their origins during slavery, include fathers whose interests are bound to the common interests of the family. Fathers in these stable families held a trusted position among whites. Burpee and the Washingtons are representatives of the second family type. Other families I mention, such as Nike's and Ericka's, represent Frazier's maternal family.

2. See Fleisher (2002).

3. Ibid.

4. See Fleisher (2001a) and Geertz (1957).

Chapter 5. New Neighbors

1. Cromwell's (1934: 31) description accurately describes the north end that I saw. "In some instances the people . . . have small flower gardens, and their yards are kept in good condition. In many of the yards, trash of all kinds may be found. Because the children have little space in the yards in which to play, they are usually found playing in a vacant field or in the streets."

Chapter 6. Dreams and Realities

1. I didn't take notes as I drove. I pulled off the road, asked questions, and captured the essence of their conversation. I sought to understand the logic of the cultural process that determines who is designated a baby daddy. It made sense that the physical location of the male was crucial; if the man was in prison at the time when the baby would have been conceived, then he couldn't be the baby daddy.

2. Frazier's history of black families documents sex and marriage patterns in clear, specific terms over the course of black history dating back to slavery. North end cultural patterns of sex and marriage conform well to Frazier's analysis. I reexamine Frazier's family types as these apply to north end patterns of

sex and marriage. My analysis challenges ethnocentric explanations of black marriage and kinship by recasting black marriage and kinship within the context of cross-cultural systems of kinship and marriage, recognizing, of course, that West African culture was the origin of these patterns later altered by pressures of the sociocultural contexts of American slavery. According to Frazier, puberty rites, bride price, bride payment, betrothal, community-prescribed marriage ceremonies, and prescriptive or proscriptive mate selection that establishes or restricts sociopolitical ties among community families are not features of black culture. The universal cultural function of marriage ascribes legitimacy to children but doesn't include coresidence and household economic goals, which are functions of particular cultures (Gough 1959). Ceremonies, rituals, economic exchanges in gift giving and elaborate wedding ceremonies are secondary to the primary function of marriage, which is to legitimize children. Marriages do function as means of displaying family wealth and thereby elevating families' community status and prestige. With or without those elaborate ceremonies, children are recognized and legitimized within a cultural community by virtue of a maternal attachment. In the black community, the term "baby mama" sufficiently defines in a public arena a child's attachment to his or her mother's family; a similar attachment to a biological father's family remains optional. A public announcement that so-and-so is a child's baby mama acts to ascribe cultural legitimacy to a child, even without white culture's expectations of legal and ceremonial displays. "Mario LaWanda baby" is all it took for Mario to become a member of the black cultural community. Frazier attributes this pattern of cultural legitimacy of children to the historical conditions of slavery. Monogamy is least well adapted to those harsh social and economic conditions (Gough 1959; Prince Peter 1955). A cultural adaptation suitable to conditions of economic scarcity includes a practice of sexual mate selection that proscribes sexual exclusivity between a woman and a man, particularly when, as Frazier notes, men are absent or offer little by way of economic support to the household. A preferable and more adaptive pattern that works to mothers' economic advantage is polyandry, a practice that was prominent in the African Congo, although thoroughly degraded as immoral by the colonial government (Prince Peter 1963). Polyandrous relations mean that it's hard to know if males or females control sexual selection; given what I've seen and heard on the north end, it's a good bet women control the flow of sex partners. There are no overt cultural limitations on a male's or female's selection of sex partners. Young women in their late teens and early twenties often have multiple children by different biological fathers and settle into their own independent living arrangements. When teenage girls become mothers they no longer hang out on the streets with mid-teenage girls without children; a withdrawal from street activity limits mothers' sexual availability. Males become part of teenage girls' personal networks early, and by age fourteen teenagers are sexually active (Fleisher 2002) and also become vulnerable to sexual exploitation, physical and emotional abuse, manipulation, and aggressive bullying instigated by males' instrumental motives, like drug selling. The average age of first sexual relations is fourteen; sixteen is the average age at which girls have their first child. Girls have an average of ten sex partners before they get pregnant for the first time. Girls who remain in school are sexually exposed to more males and become pregnant more quickly and more often than girls who drop out. Teenage and young-adult mothers have preferential sex partners. Gang affiliation, either a woman's or a man's, does not influence sexual pair bonding.

3. Frazier's (1937) analysis of maternal families begs a broader cross-cultural interpretation of the black kinship system. All kinship systems are designed to create social order (Barnes 1981; Jones 2010; Kullanda 2002). Kinship systems' terminology classifies people into a finite number of categories: there are blood relatives, relatives by marriage, and nonrelatives; what makes a person a blood relative is a function of cultural categorizations, not DNA. Kin are defined by closeness (siblings) or distance (cousins, nephews, nieces). These categories are arranged into groups, which are further broken down into generational kin — parents, aunts, uncles — and lineal kin — mothers, fathers, grandparents, great-grandparents, and so on. It's hard to classify people into kinship categories like these if a culture doesn't practice monogamy or serial monogamy and if a culture doesn't prescribe marriage ceremonies and if it proscribes polyandrous relationships. Kinship terms and categories are more than social labels: they are cognitive categories (Jones 2010). That means social structure, social cognition, and language are inextricably linked and influence cultural worldview. A culture's kinship categories structure relationships and organize ascribed patterns of culturally determined social roles and responsibilities. A culture that allows polyandrous relations rules out paternity debates. Women in the north end don't tend to file a paternity claim in local courts when the baby daddies fail to provide social and economic support, nor do fathers or mothers of pregnant teens bang on the doors of their daughter's alleged biological fathers demanding financial compensation. "Why bother?," women asked who had demanded or expected their baby daddy to sign a birth certificate and were sorely disappointed when they failed to appear at the hospital. Black culture is historically ambivalent when it comes to public recognition of children's biological fathers and their potential social involvement in children's lives. If baby daddies help in some way, that's fine. If they don't,

that's fine, too. The responsibility of child rearing, as Byron declared, belongs to baby mamas. Kinship and marriage in black culture does not operate on a full playing field of functionally active consanguineal and affinal kin who can afford to support or give access to material, financial, or affective resources.

The absence of socially recognized biological paternity creates ambiguity among potential affinal kinship ties that have either few or unknown social referents. In natural conversations, I never heard anyone use an expression "She's my mother-in-law." A man does not use the term "mother-in-law" as an honorific to refer to his female partner's mother or his baby mama's mama. The terms "uncle" and "father" are rarely if ever heard in natural conversations. A teenager might use the term "daddy" to refer to a friendly adult or an older close or best friend.

Natural conversations include terms that describe the most dominant socially determined kinship relations: "mama," "gramma," "auntie," and to a lesser degree "cousin." A child-focused generational kinship system operates through kinship terms that embed children within a network of caretakers in the new baby mama's generation or an ascending generation. Each generation's mamas, grammas, and aunties are culturally prescribed caretakers. Every baby mama has social ties to caretakers in the form of mama, gramma, and aunties. Mothers, grammas, and aunties, whether these are biological or fictive, share children and are shared by children. Cousins are problematic within the black kinship system, obscured by an absence of determination of paternity and biological ties among a child's mama and her brothers and sisters. If biological fathers remain unknown, then cousins determined through the biological tie between a father and his siblings are biologically undetermined. Black culture's generational kinship system puts a high value on children within the same age grade. Children who call one another cousins might be cousins with a known origin in biologically determined kinship, or they might use the term "cousin" to indicate a close social relationship or fictive biological kin. In either case, a cousin relation establishes a close social bond, and with that bond comes social responsibilities.

On the north end, the prefix "step" is an irregular addition to the socially recognized kinship system, seemingly imposed by bureaucratic obligations outside the community. If a mother has a live-in, cross-sex relationship, the mother's children do not address her male partner as "dad" or refer to him as a stepfather in natural conversations. Step relations are recognized by adolescents outside of natural conversations if they are asked to specify their relationships to others in their age grade to outsiders, like a researcher or a government employee. Schools, government agencies, and the legal system require more precise social classifications. Step relations are thoroughly ambiguous and can apply to just about anyone when needed. On the north end, a stepparent does not have culturally recognized social obligations toward a stepchild, and a stepchild does not recognize culturally determined social obligations of a stepparent toward them. My experience in gathering kinship terms is that step relations are obscure to informants, particularly if informants are asked to identify how they are specifically linked to step relatives.

A kinship system that lacks a need to impose legal obligations of paternity on social relations has a less instrumental need for the use of given last names. People know their own last name, although the derivation of that name from a biological father or social origin can remain unclear, particularly in cases when families' biological ties have been distorted by drug abuse, imprisonment, domestic violence, and female household head's multiple live-in, opposite-sex partners. Personal naming practices can get confusing (Fleisher 2002). Given last names were more frequently unknown than known among friends. Even among close friends, given first names were often unknown. Nicknames were common and well known in the neighborhood. In cases when two or three girls had the same given first name, girls I interviewed in the social network study had difficulty distinguishing among them. In a case when there were three Vice Lord girls named Niece, I had to distinguish among them. I asked for distinguishing traits. Girls used traits, singularly or in combination, like height, age, weight, skin color shade, and hair color.

4. Friends linked to friends who are linked to other friends formed a network of friends (Fleisher 2002). Young women who didn't have children had friendship networks that ranged in size from five to thirty-two; the average age of the friends was eighteen. Each woman had an average of nine female and four male friends. Young women with children had networks that ranged in size from three to twenty-nine; the average age of the people in these networks was twenty-two. Each woman had an average of eight female and one male friend. Friendship ties compensate for few culturally determined kinship ties; friendships bind people by degree and category; these friends are dispersed over a geographic area, making resources available like ATMs at shopping malls across a city. There are no specific terms that differentiate a friend and a close friend and a best friend. Young women rely on friends in their generation, like Ericka did, as their sole source of social, economic, and emotional support. Friends are the principal resource shared among young women with and without children. A need for close friendship bonds becomes imperative among young mothers. Young mothers' closest friends are young mothers. Young mothers are linked to older women. Older women are mothers, too, and along

with daughters and their children form an intergenerational structural system for child care and social, economic, and instrumental support.

Chapter 7. Rebirth Days

1. When I was employed by the north central regional office of Federal Bureau of Prisons in the regional case management department, among other duties, I designated inmates to federal prisons.
2. See Dundes (1969, 1971).
3. See Felder (1988).
4. See Fleisher and Krienert (2009).
5. See Fleisher and Krienert (2004).

Chapter 8. They Don't Need a Savior

1. See Atkinson, Delamont, and Housley (2008) and White (1980).
2. See Geertz (1973, 1988) and Fleisher (2001a).
3. See Geertz (1974).
4. See Geertz (1988), R. A. Levine (1966), S. Levine (1979), McLaughlin (1981), and Tobin (1986).
5. See Harvey and Reed (1996).
6. See Lipsey and Cordray (2000).
7. See Fleisher (1998).

Epilogue

1. The phrase "insufficiencies in property" was coined by my son, Aaron Michel Fleisher, who studied philosophy at the University of Chicago and earned a master's degree in library and information science from the University of Illinois, Urbana-Champaign. I refer to Aaron in several places and want to recognize his contribution to this book. He regularly visited the north end with me before his first year at the University of Chicago and subsequently accompanied me when he was home from college on vacation. Aaron and Burpee were good friends. Aaron insisted on providing north end families with Christmas gifts. Burpee wanted a bike so he could ride around the neighborhood and watch the goings on and sneak up on and chastise youngsters selling weed. Aaron gave his bike to Burpee. Aaron read many of the earliest drafts of portions of this manuscript and contributed his depth of knowledge of America's racial history and his thorough knowledge of the philosophical underpinnings of the

ethnographic method and challenged the ways I described people and places and underlying arguments about poverty, race, and discrimination. Aaron helped shape my thinking about how best to tell the story of the north end, the Washington family, and Burpee's family.

2. See Cutler and Glaeser (1999) and Nesbit (1926).

3. See Cromwell (1934) and Bindman (1961).

4. It's worth considering that the negative traits that whites attributed to black migrants became embedded in historical narratives about black migrants (see White 1980, 2009), which later resurfaced in white folkloric characterizations of the north end as a "jungle."

References

Allison, T. W. 1924. "Population Movements in Chicago." *Journal of Social Forces* 2: 529–33.

Angel, R. J., and M. Tienda. 1982. "Determinants of Extended Household Structure: Cultural Pattern or Economic Need?" *American Journal of Sociology* 87: 1360–83.

Arewa, E., and A. Dundes. 1964. "Proverbs and the Ethnography of Speaking Folklore." *American Anthropologist* 66: 70–85.

Atkinson, P., S. Delamont, and W. Housley. 2008. *Contours of Culture: Complex Ethnography and the Ethnography of Complexity*. Walnut Creek, CA: AltaMira Press.

Barnes, A. S. 1981. "The Black Kinship System." *Phylon* 42: 369–80.

Becker, H. S., and B. Geer. 1957. "Participant Observation and Interviewing: A Comparison." *Human Organization* 16: 28–32.

Benford, R. A. 2002. "Controlling Narratives and Narratives as Control within Social Movements." In *Stories of Change: Narrative and Social Movements*, edited by J. E. Davis, 53–75. Albany: State University of New York Press.

Benford, R. A., and D. A. Snow. 2000. "Framing Processes and Social Movements: An Overview and Assessment." *Annual Review of Sociology* 26: 611–39.

Bindman, A. M. 1961. "Minority Collective Action against Local Discrimination: A Study of the Negro Community in Champaign-Urbana, Illinois." Master's thesis, University of Illinois, Urbana-Champaign.

———. 1965. "Interviewing in the Search for 'Truth.'" *Sociological Quarterly* 6: 281–85.

Bossler, A.M. 2004. "The Employment Status Dichotomy: Understanding What This Means and Using It." In *Crime and Employment: Critical Issues in Crime Reduction for Corrections*, edited by J. L. Krienert and M. S. Fleisher, 13-38. Walnut Creek, CA: AltaMira Press.

Chatters, L. M., R. J. Taylor, and H. W. Neighbors. 1989. "Size of the Informal Network Mobilized in Response to Serious Personal Problems." *Journal of Marriage and the Family* 51: 667-76.

Cromwell, J. A. 1934. "History and Organization of the Negro Community in Champaign-Urbana, Illinois." Master's thesis, University of Illinois, Urbana-Champaign.

Cutler, D. M., and E. L. Glaeser. 1999. "The Rise and Decline of the American Ghetto." *Journal of Political Economy* 107: 455-505.

Dundes, A. 1965. "The Study of Folklore in Literature and Culture: Identification and Interpretation." *Journal of American Folklore* 78: 136-42.

———. 1969. "Thinking Ahead: A Folkloristic Reflection of the Future Orientation in American Worldview." *Anthropological Quarterly* 42: 53-72.

———. 1971. "Folk Ideas as Units of Worldview." *Journal of American Folklore* 84: 93-103.

Espelage, D., S. Wasserman, and M. S. Fleisher. 2007. "Social Networks and Violent Behavior." In *Cambridge Handbook of Violent Behavior*, edited by D. J. Flannery, A. Vazsonyi, and I. Waldman, 450-64. New York: Cambridge University Press.

Felder, R. M. 1988. "How Students Learn: Adapting Teaching Styles to Learning Styles." *Proceedings of the Frontiers of Education Conference*: 489-93.

Fine G. A., and I. Khawaja. 2005. "Celebrating Arabs and Grateful Terrorists: Rumor and the Politics of Plausibility." In *Rumor Mills: The Social Impact of Rumor and Legend*, edited by G. A. Fine, V. Campion-Vincent, and C. Heath, 189-205. New Brunswick, NJ: Transaction.

Flannery, D. J., and J. M. Kretschmar. 2012. "Fugitive Safe Surrender." *Criminology and Public Policy* 11: 437-59.

Fleisher, M. S. 1976. "Clallam: A Study in Coast Salish Ethnolinguistics." *Language Description Heritage: An Open Access Digital Library.* ldh.clld.org/1976/01/01/escidoc400984/.

———. 1989. *Warehousing Violence.* Newbury Park, CA: Sage.

———. 1995. *Beggars and Thieves: Lives of Urban Street Criminals.* Madison: University of Wisconsin Press.

———. 1998. *Dead End Kids: Gang Girls and the Boys They Know.* Madison: University of Wisconsin Press.

———. 2000a. "Issues in Offender Reentry: Street-up Planning for Male and Female Offenders." Federal Bureau of Prisons, Offender Workgroup, invited speaker, September, Washington, DC.

———. 2000b. "Reentry and Reintegration of Imprisoned Gang Members." Youth Gang Consortium of Federal Agencies (HUD, DOE, HHS, FBI, BJS, ATF), May 30, Washington, DC.

———. 2001a. "(Counter-)transference and Compassion Fatigue in Gang Ethnography." *Focaal* 36: 77–94.

———. 2001b. "Residential Mobility of Adult Male Gang Members." Final Report to the U.S. Census Bureau for the Comparative Ethnographic Research on Mobile Populations Project.

———. 2002. *Women and Gangs.* U.S. Department of Justice, Office of Juvenile Justice and Delinquency Prevention, Washington, DC.

———. 2003. "From Jail to Lecture Hall." TheConnection.org, National Public Radio, Boston, August 13.

———. 2009. "Coping with Structural Adversity: Poverty, Gangs and Resilience in a U.S. African-American Urban Community." *Journal of Contingencies and Crisis Management* 17: 274–84.

Fleisher, M. S., and J. L. Krienert. 2004. "Drug Selling: A Rational Choice." In *Crime and Employment: Critical Issues in Crime Reduction for Corrections,* edited by J. L. Krienert and M. S. Fleisher, 192–210. Walnut Creek, CA: AltaMira Press.

———. 2009. *The Myth of Prison Rape: Sexual Culture in American Prisons.* Lanham, MD: Rowman and Littlefield.

Fleisher, M. S., and A. V. Papachristos. 2010. "Social Network Analysis and Ethnography: Complementary Tools to Understand the Complexities of Real-life Behavior." Paper presented at the International Network of Social Network Analysts Conference, July, Riva del Garda, Italy.

Foster, G. M. 1953. "What Is Folk Culture?" *American Anthropologist* 55: 159–73.

Frazier, E. F. 1937. "The Impact of Urban Civilization upon Negro Family Life." *American Sociological Review* 2: 609–18.

Friedenberg, E. Z. 1962. "Voices of Poverty." *Commentary* (January) www.commentarymagazine.

Geertz, C. 1957. "Ethos, World-view and the Analysis of Sacred Symbols." *Antioch Review* 17: 421–37.

———. 1973. "Thick Description: Toward an Interpretive Theory of Culture." In *The Interpretation of Cultures: Selected Essays,* 3–30. New York: Basic Books.

———. 1974. "'From the Native's Point of View': On the Nature of Anthropological Understanding." *Bulletin of the American Academy of Arts and Sciences* 28: 26–45.

———. 1988. *Works and Lives: Anthropologist as Author*. Stanford, CA: Stanford University Press.

Gough, K. E. 1959. "Is the Family Universal? The Nayar Case." *Journal of Royal Anthropological Institute* 89: 23–34.

Harvey, D. L., and M. H. Reed. 1996. "The Culture of Poverty: An Ideological Analysis." *Sociological Perspectives* 39: 465–95.

Hill, R. 1997. *The Strengths of African American Families: Twenty-Five Years Later*. Washington, DC: R and B Publishers.

Hughes, E. C. 1954. "Robert E. Park's Views on Urban Society: A Comment on William L. Kolb's Paper." *Economic Development and Cultural Change* 3: 47–49.

Hughes, L. A. 2005. "Studying Youth Gangs: Alternative Methods and Conclusions." *Journal of Contemporary Criminal Justice* 21: 98–119.

———. 2006. "Studying Youth Gangs: The Importance of Context." In *Studying Youth Gangs*, edited by J. F. Short and L. A. Hughes, 37–45. Walnut Creek, CA: AltaMira.

Institute for Intergovernmental Research. 2009. *OJJDP Comprehensive Gang Model: Planning for Implementation*. Retrieved from www.nationalgang center.gov.

Irwin, J. 1970. *The Felon*. Englewood Cliffs, NJ: Prentice-Hall.

———. 2005. *The Warehouse Prison*. Los Angeles, CA: Roxbury.

Jackson, W. C. 1923. "The Negro Offender." *Journal of Social Forces* 1: 147–48.

Jacobs, J. B. 1978. *Stateville: The Penitentiary in Mass Society*. Chicago: University of Chicago Press.

Jones, D. 2010. "Human Kinship, from Conceptual Structure to Grammar." *Behavioral and Brain Sciences* 33: 367–416.

Kemp, B. 2009. "Bloomington Was the Scene for Lincoln's Famous 'Lost Speech.'" *Pantagraph*, February 14. Retrieved from www.pantagraph.com.

Kullanda, S. 2002. "Indo-European 'Kinship Terms' Revisited." *Current Anthropology* 43: 89–111.

Kusmer, K. L. 1978. *A Ghetto Takes Shape: Black Cleveland, 1870–1930*. Champaign: University of Illinois Press.

Labov, W. 1972. *Language in the Inner City: Studies in the Black English Vernacular*. Philadelphia: University of Pennsylvania Press.

Levine, R. A. 1966. *Dreams and Deeds*. Chicago: University of Chicago Press.

Levine, S. 1979. *Mothers and Wives: Gusii Women of East Africa.* Chicago: University of Chicago Press.

Lewis, O. 1950. "An Anthropological Approach to Family Studies." *American Journal of Sociology* 55: 468-75.

———. 1951. *Life in a Mexican Village: Tepoztlan Restudied.* Champaign: University of Illinois Press.

———. 1952. "Urbanization without Breakdown: A Case Study." *Scientific Monthly* 75: 31-41.

———. 1961. *Children of Sanchez: Autobiography of a Mexican Family.* New York: Random House.

———. 1998. "The Culture of Poverty." *Society* 35: 7-9.

Lind, A. W. 1930. "The Ghetto and the Slum." *Social Forces* 9: 206-15.

Lipsey, M. W., and D. S. Cordray. 2000. "Evaluation Methods for Social Intervention." *Annual Review of Psychology* 51: 345-75.

Lynch, J. P., and W. J. Sabol. 2001. *Prisoner Reentry in Perspective.* Crime Policy Report 3, September. Washington, DC: Urban Institute.

Malinowski, B. 1922. *Argonauts of the Western Pacific.* New York: Dutton.

Marks, C. 1989. *Farewell—We're Good and Gone: The Great Black Migration.* Bloomington: Indiana University Press.

Masotti, L. H., and J. R. Corsi. 1969. *Shoot-Out in Cleveland: Black Militants and the Police.* Washington, DC: Government Printing Office.

Mayhew, B. H. 1983. "Causality, Historical Particularism and Other Errors in Sociological Discourse." *Journal for the Theory of Social Behavior* 13: 285-300.

McLaughlin, J. T. 1981. "Transference, Psychic Reality, and Countertransference." *Psychoanalytic Quarterly* 59: 639-64.

Miller, W. B. 1958. "Lower Class Culture as a Generating Milieu of Gang Delinquency." *Journal of Social Issues* 14: 5-19.

———. 1962. "Cultural Features of an Urban Lower Class Community." National Institute of Mental Health, Community Services Branch, Silver Spring, Maryland.

Nesbit, F. 1926. "Cause of Some Failures in the Work of the United Charities of Chicago." *Social Forces* 5: 258-68.

Newbold, G., and J. I. Ross. 2012. "Convict Criminology at the Crossroads: Research Note." *Prison Journal* 93: 3-10.

Olzak, S., S. Shanahan, and E. H. McEneaney. 1996. "Poverty, Segregation, and Race Riots: 1960 to 1993." *American Sociological Review* 61: 590-613.

Park, R. E. 1915. "The City: Suggestions for the Investigation of Human Behavior in the City Environment." *American Journal of Sociology* 20: 577-612.

Petersilia, J. 2003. *When Prisoners Come Home: Parole and Prisoner Reentry.* New York: Oxford University Press.

Pew Center on the States. 2011. *State of Recidivism: The Revolving Door of America's Prisons.* Washington, DC: Pew Charitable Trusts.

Price-Spratlen, T. 1998. "Between Depression and Prosperity? Changes in the Community Context of Historical African American Migration." *Social Forces* 77: 515–39.

Prince Peter of Greece and Denmark. 1955. "Polyandry and Kinship Group." *Man* 55: 1179–81.

———. 1963. *A Study of Polyandry.* The Hague: Mouton.

Sandven, K., and M. D. Resnick. 1990. "Informal Adoption among Black Adolescent Mothers." *American Journal of Orthopsychiatry* 60: 210–24.

Short, J. F., and L. A. Hughes, eds. 2006. *Studying Youth Gangs.* Walnut Creek, CA: AltaMira.

Short, J. F., and F. L. Strodtbeck. 1965. *Group Process and Gang Delinquency.* Chicago: University of Chicago Press.

Spergel, I. A. 1995. *The Youth Gang Problem.* New York: Oxford University Press.

Spiro, M. E. 1986. "Cultural Relativism and the Future of Anthropology." *Cultural Anthropology* 1: 259–86.

Spradley, J. P. 1970. *You Owe Yourself a Drunk: Adaptive Strategies of Urban Nomads.* Boston: Little, Brown.

Stack, C. B. 1975. *All Our Kin: Strategies for Survival in a Black Community.* New York: Basic Books.

Stewart, W. A. 1967. "Sociolinguistic Factors in the History of American Negro Dialects." In *Readings in African American Language,* edited by N. Norment Jr., 77–88. New York: Peter Lang.

Taylor, R. J. 1990. "Need for Support and Family Involvement among Black Americans." *Journal of Marriage and the Family* 52: 584–90.

Tobin, J. J. 1986. "(Counter)transference and Failure in Intercultural Therapy." *Ethnos* 14: 120–43.

Travis, J., and S. Lawrence. 2002. *Beyond the Prison Gates: The State of Parole in America.* Washington, DC: Urban Institute.

Travis, J., A. L. Solomon, and M. Waul. 2001. *From Prison to Home: The Dimensions and Consequences of Prisoner Reentry.* Washington, DC: Urban Institute.

Wasserman, S., and K. Faust. 1994. *Social Network Analysis: Methods and Applications.* Cambridge: Cambridge University Press.

White, H. 1980. "The Value of Narrativity in the Representation of Reality." *Critical Inquiry* 7: 5–27.

———. 2009. *The Content of the Form: Narrative Discourse and Historical Representation*. Baltimore, MD: Johns Hopkins University Press.

Whyte, W. F. 1943. *Street Corner Society*. Chicago: University of Chicago Press.

Wilson. 1987. *The Truly Disadvantaged: The Inner City, the Underclass, and Public Policy*. Chicago: University of Chicago Press.

Wirth, L., ed. 1928. *The Ghetto*. Chicago: University of Chicago Press.

Zorbaugh, H. W. 1983 [1929]. *The Gold Coast and the Slum: A Sociological Study of Chicago's Near North Side*. Chicago: University of Chicago Press.